C. M. Ingleby

Shakespeare; The Man and the Book

Being a Collection of Occasional Papers on the Bard and his Writings - Part the First

C. M. Ingleby

Shakespeare; The Man and the Book
Being a Collection of Occasional Papers on the Bard and his Writings - Part the First

ISBN/EAN: 9783337063450

Printed in Europe, USA, Canada, Australia, Japan

Cover: Foto ©ninafisch / pixelio.de

More available books at **www.hansebooks.com**

SHAKESPEARE

The Man and The Book:

Being a Collection of Occasional Papers on the Bard
and his Writings.

Part the First.

BY

C. M. INGLEBY, M.A., LL.D., V.P.R.S.L.

LONDON:
Printed by JOSIAH ALLEN, of Birmingham,
& Published by TRÜBNER & Co., 57 & 59, Ludgate Hill.
1877.
[All Rights Reserved.]

Contents.

	PAGE
Note	i

SHAKESPEARE THE MAN.

Chapter I.—The Spelling of the Surname	1
Chapter II.—The Meaning of the Surname	12
Chapter III.—Shakespeare's Traditional Birthday	21
Postscript. On certain Annotated Copies of Langbaine's *Account*	36
Chapter IV.—The Authorship of the Works attributed to Shakespeare	38
Chapter V.—The Portraiture of Shakespeare (Recent Contributions to)	73
Chapter VI.—Matters Personal to Shakespeare	92
Intercalary Notes and Corrections	103

SHAKESPEARE THE BOOK.

Chapter VII.—The Modern Prometheus	107
Chapter VIII.—The Idiosyncrasy of Hamlet	120
Chapter IX.—Some Passages Reprieved	137
Chapter X.—The Soule Arayed	153
Intercalary Notes	169

Note.

MICHAEL Faraday, in a letter to Mary Somerville under date 17th January, 1859, wrote, 'It is useful to get one's scattered papers together, with an index.' This is my reason for issuing the ensuing collection, of which three papers are reprinted from the *Transactions* of the Royal Society of Literature.

I have excluded from it all reviews of books, besides seven articles on Shakespearian matters, contributed by me to *The Birmingham Gazette*, *The Englishman's Magazine*, and *Once a Week*, which I did not consider worthy of republication. As to those constituting this instalment, I may honestly say, that, with the exception of the penultimate chapter, it is not likely either reader or reviewer will take a more modest estimate of their value than their author. That chapter has somewhat higher pretensions, for it is devoted to the defense of Shakespeare's text in five passages which are usually emended in modern editions.

The chapter on Recent Contributions to 'the Portraiture of Shakespeare' was written as a descriptive commentary on a collection of portraits exhibited at a meeting of the above-mentioned Society, and apart from them can have but little interest.

SHAKESPEARE:
THE MAN AND THE BOOK.

—o—

CHAPTER I.

THE SPELLING OF THE SURNAME.

AMIDST the many discrepant literal forms in which our great poet's surname is given by hand-writers, we have, as it seems to us, to adopt that which was usually employed by his contemporaries. Mr. Halliwell tells us (*Life of Shakespeare*, 1848), p. 281, that it is

a matter of great uncertainty whether Shakespeare was one of the few persons of the time who adopted a uniform orthography in his signature; but, on the supposition that he always wrote his name SHAKSPERE, it was contended as early as 1784 that it should be printed in this curtalled form. The question is one of very small importance, and the only circumstance worth consideration in the matter is the tendency of this innovation to introduce [or revive] the pronunciation SHAXPERE, a piece of affectation so far dangerous, inasmuch as it harmonizes not with the beautiful lines that have been consecrated to his memory by Ben Jonson and other eminent poets;* and those who have adopted it seem to have overlooked the fact, that in the orthography of proper names the printed literature of the day is the only safe criterion. In the case of Shakespeare, there are the poems of *Lucrece* and *Venus and Adonis*, published under his own superintendence, in which [*i. e.*, both on the title-pages and in the Dedicatory Epistles] the name occurs as SHAKESPEARE, and so it is found in almost every work printed in the lifetime of the poet. * * [Besides he] was called SHAKESPEARE by his literary friends.

* In this mention of 'Ben Jonson and other eminent poets,' the allusion is, among other, to the lines:

>   Looke how the father's face
>   Lives in his issue, even so, the race
>   Of Shakespeare's minde and manners brightly shines
>   In his well torned, and true-filed lines:
>   In each of which, he seems to *shake a lance*,
>   As brandish't at the eyes of Ignorance.

To shake or brandish the spear was a menacing gesture preceding the actual delivery of the weapon. Cf. Spenser's *Faery Queen*, b. iv, c. iii, st. 10.

>   He, all enraged, his quivering *speare* did *shake*,
>   And charging him afresh thus felly him bespake:

and *Histrio-mastix, or the Player Whipt*, 4to, 1610 (Sig. C. 4 *recto*).

>   Thy knight his valiant elboe weares,
>   That when he *shakes* his furious *Speare*,
>   The foe in shivering fearfull sort,
>   May lay him downe in death to snort:

in which the late lamented Mr. Richard Simpson saw an allusion to Shakespeare. (New Shakspere Society's *Transactions*, 1874, p. 391.) Besides, the style which alone forms a basis for this conceit is that uniformly adopted by the writers of commendatory verses (with scarcely an exception), some half dozen of whom give the name Shake-speare (*i. e.*, with the hyphen) as if to emphasise the pronunciation.

There is a similar conceit in the 119th Epigram of Thomas Bancroft (1639).

>   To Shakespeare.
>   Thou hast so us'd thy *Pen* (or shooke thy Speare),
>   That Poets startle, nor thy wit come neare.

On this point Mr. Halliwell's decision is identical with that arrived at sixteen years later by M. Victor Hugo. He does indeed, as is usual with him, commit some inaccuracies in dealing with the question of the orthography: he states one document to be extant which ceased to be so at some time in the seventeenth century, and another to have been lost, which is always exposed to public view in the Department of Manuscripts of the British Museum; but his verdict is substantially right, and is well expressed. It runs thus (*William Shakespeare*, 1864):*

> There is little agreement on the orthography of the word Shake-speare, as a family name: it is written variously—Shakspere, Shakespere, Shakespeare, Shakspeare;† in the eighteenth century it was habitually written Shakespear; the present translator [M. François Victor Hugo] has adopted the spelling Shakespeare, as the only true method, and gives for it unanswerable reasons. The only objection that can be made is that Shakspeare is more easily pronounced than Shakespeare, that cutting off the e mute is perhaps useful, and that for their own sake, and in the interests of literary currency, posterity has, as regards surnames, a claim to euphony. It is evident, for example, that in French poetry the orthography Shakspeare is necessary. However, in prose, and convinced by the translator, we write Shakespeare.

There is little to be excepted to here, save (perhaps) 'the only objection.' That indeed is defensible from M. Victor

---

* We cannot give this extract our approbation, without adding our censure on the book. Probably, never in the whole course of biographical literature, were so many ridiculous mistakes and culpable blunders brought together in a single volume devoted to a single mind as in this strange rhapsody. A further accession of blunders came in with M. A. Baillot's wretched English version, which invests the French rhapsodist with a Nessus-shirt of solecisms.

† And in fifty other forms: see pp. 6-8.

Hugo's own point of view; he believing that Shakespeare's dedication to Lord Southampton of *Venus and Adonis* is extant in Shakespeare's autograph. We heartily wish that belief were as true as it is new: for there, as in the Dedication to the same patron of *Lucrece*, we have the full style of SHAKESPEARE. We go thus far with the great French romancer: we believe both dedications were set up from Shakespeare's autograph; and we therefore hold the spelling, as such, to be entitled to as much respect as any of those which we possess in Shakespeare's autograph. But it is on quite other grounds that we give the preference to the full style in publicly dealing with his life and works. It is the one style uniformly sanctioned by the press of his own day. All the title-pages of the first quarto editions of his separate plays, with one exception, have the surname in that style, or not at all. The exception is *Love's Labour's Lost*, 1598, where the name is given SHAKESPERE. In the title-page of *Hamlet*, 1603, it is SHAKE-SPEARE: and in those of *Hamlet*, 1604, &c., *Much Adoe About Nothing*, 1600; *A Midsommer Night's Dreame*, 1600 (both editions); *The Merchant of Venice*, 1600 (both editions); *The Second Part of Henrie the Fourth*, 1600; *Syr John Falstaffe, and the Merrie Wives of Windsor*, 1602; *The Famous Historie of Troylus and Cresseid*, 1609 (both editions); *Pericles, Prince of Tyre*, 1609, and *Othello*, 1622, the name is uniformly SHAKESPEARE. In the case of the remaining eight earliest quartos, the name of the author does not appear. All the folio editions concur in giving the same orthography. Surely such a concurrence of testimony is overwhelming; and what evidence have we to set against it?

Mr. F. J. Furnivall, the Founder and Director of 'The New Shakspere Society,' in his 'Prospectus,' adopts the spelling SHAKSPERE, and attempts to justify it in the following foot-note.

This spelling of our great Poet's name is taken from the only unquestionably genuine signatures of his that we possess, the three on his will, and the two on his Stratford conveyance and mortgage. None of these signatures have an *e* after the *k* ;* four have no *a* after the first *e* ; the fifth I read *-eere*. The *e* and *a* had their French sounds, which explain the forms 'Shaxper,' &c. Though it has hitherto been too much to ask people to suppose that SHAKSPERE knew how to spell his own name, I hope the demand may not prove too great for the imagination of the Members of the New Society.

With the facts before us, we are at a loss to account for the sarcasm of the final sentence. The concession asked for, 'that Shakespeare knew how to spell his own name,' conveys a sophism, which ought not to have imposed on many: and which we take the liberty of exposing for the benefit of the few. In Shakespeare's time there was no such a thing as the orthography, or correct spelling, of a man's name. One or two (as Burghley, perhaps), as far as we know, used one literal form ; but the rule is the other way. Every man spelt his name, and his neighbour's name, as best reconciled his eye and ear; and

* The second sentence thus stood in the earlier proofs : 'None of these signatures have an *e* after the *k*, or an *a* after the first *e*.'
Then it stood thus : 'None of these signatures have an *e* after the *k* : four have *a* after the first *e* ; the fifth I read *-eere*.'
Of these earlier versions, the second, through a misprint, is logically inconsistent with the first sentence of the foot-note. Of the later versions, the words, 'the fifth I read *-eere*' is but the record of a mistake, which, indeed, has been made before, but ought not to blemish the 'Prospectus' of 'The New Shakspere Society.'

in the case of some prominent persons we have nearly a dozen different spellings of one surname. Thus we have **Jonson**, Johnson, Jhonson : Henslow (or with the *e* final), Henslo, Hensley, Henchley, Hinchlow (or with the *e* final), Hinchley, Inclow, &c. ; Raleigh, Rauley, Rawleigh, Rawlegh, Rawley, &c. ; Decker, Dekker, Dickers, &c. ; Hall, Hawle, &c.; and so forth : and if one thing be more certain than another, it is this, that, as a rule, no one used a single literal form of any surname—his own, or that of another.

Mr. Halliwell pointed out, in 1848 (*Life of Shakespeare*, p. 282), the absurdity of erecting any one autograph of a man's name into a standard. Unquestionably some, probably all, of the five signatures of Shakespeare are SHAKSPERE; and certainly none of them has the *e* after the *k:* yet Gilbert Shakespeare, the bard's brother, spelt his own name SHAKESPERE. We have no doubt whatever that if we had access to a large number of signatures by members of the family, we should find all sorts of spellings, and that every one adopted several forms of the name on different occasions.

To judge from the documents from which Mr. Halliwell gives quotations, or which he prints at length, the family of our bard had a pretty extensive assortment of literal forms to choose from. We find most of the following many times repeated :

1450 to 1550.

Schakespeire.	Shakespeyre.
Schakespere.	Shakespeyr.
Schakspere.	Shakspere.
Chacsper.	Shakespere.

1550 to 1650.

Shakspere. { Shaxpere.   Saxpere.
              Shaxspere. Saxspere. *

Shaksper. { Shaxper.   Saxsper (?).
              Shaxsper.

Shakspeare.   Shaxpeare.
Shakspear (?).   Shaxpear (?).
Shakspeere.   Shaxpeere (?).
Shakspeer.   Shaxpeer.
Shakspeyre.
Shakspeyr.
Shackspeare.
Shackspear.
Shackspere.   Shakxspere (?).   Shaxkspere.
Shacksper.   Shakxsper.   Shaxksper (?).
Shackspeer (?).
Shackspeere.
Shackspire.
Shakespere.   Shaxepere (?).   Shaxkespere.   Shagspere.
Shakesper.
Shakespeere.   ⎫
Shakespeer (?).   ⎪
Shakeseper.   ⎪
Shackespeare.   ⎬ Shaxeper.   Shaxkesper (?).   Sackesper.
Shackespear (?). ⎪
Shackespere.   ⎪
Shackesper.   ⎭

* The Registers of Snitterfield, 1596-7, record the burial of 'Margret *Saxpere*, widow, being times the wyff of Henry *Shakspere*.' Doubtless, to the eyes of the scribe, the one literal form was fully as adequate as the other. There was *no* orthography in those days, *pace* Mr. Furnivall.

Shakispere.
Shakisper (?).
Shakyspare.
Shakysper.
Shakuspeare:

and half a dozen other forms in which an *h* follows the *p*.*

This very curious variation occurs occasionally both in print and in manuscript. In the deed under which Shakespeare purchased, for £440, the unexpired term in a moiety of the tithes of Stratford, Old Stratford, Bishopton, and Welcombe, we find SHAKESPEARE once: SHAKESPEAR once: once he is simply initialed: and in the remaining ten cases the name appears with the second *h*: viz.,

> SHACKESPHERE thrice,
> SHAKESPHERE five times,
> SHACKSPHARE once,
> and SHAKSPHERE once.

In some editions of Camden's *Remaines concerning Britaine*, *e.g.*, the edd. of 1614 and 1637, the name, which occurs but once, is SHAKESPHEARE. In Edward Phillips' *Theatrum Poetarum*, 1675, we find SHAKESPEAR four times, and SHAKESPHEAR twice. In Milton's epitaph on the bard, as it appears in the *Poems* of 1640, the name is SHEAKESPEARE: a form we do not

---

* We have appended (?) to those spellings which have not been verified. Most of them will assuredly be found in documents of the relative period. Besides the above-recorded forms of spelling our bard's surname, there are several perversions of it which resulted from wantonness or accident. In the Cunningham forgeries of the Revels-books of 1605, we have *Shaxberd* four times: and in the French translation of Mrs. Montagu's *Essay*, printed in 1777, the surname appears on the title-page as *Sakespeart!*

remember to have seen elsewhere. From this *resumé* it would be little less than miraculous, if we did find the immediate family of Shakespeare employing only one form of spelling!

We must add that Mr. Halliwell (p. 283) gives a fac-simile of an endorsement on the indenture of 1602, between Combes and Shakespeare, which he reads

'Combe to SHACKSPEARE,' &c.,

just as (p. 109) we find Judith's name spelt *for her* on the deed of 1611.

Mr. Halliwell sees sufficient resemblance between this manuscript surname and the second and third signatures to Shakespeare's will, to support 'an argument in favour of the appropriation of the above to Shakespeare [*i.e.*, of the inference that it is his autograph], and of the correctness of reading SHAKSPEARE in those two autographs.' Apart from the question of such a resemblance, we contend that the two last signatures to the will are not SHAKSPEARE, but, like Malone's tracing of the first (now partly obliterated), SHAKSPERE. Moreover, to our eyes, the name in the endorsement of 1602 is quite unmistakeably SHACKSPERE. There is a German *r*, made wide open like a *v* (as was then the custom in cursives), between two *e*'s made like *o*'s, in the fashion then and long afterwards prevalent, the latter straggling out into a flourish. In judging of the three signatures to the will, we have not wholly relied upon the decision of our late valued friend, Sir Frederic Madden : though his decision was that of the most accomplished palæographic expert of his day, to which Mr. Furnivall might be expected to bow with deference. However, we will append his own remarks on all five signatures. We quote from his pamphlet *Observations on an Autograph of Shakspere, and the Orthography of his Name*, 1837, pp. 11-14.

The first of these signatures [*i.e.*, to the will], subscribed on the first sheet, at the right-hand corner of the paper, is decidedly WILLIAM SHAKSPERE, and no one has ventured to raise a doubt respecting the six last letters.* The second signature is at the left-hand corner of the second sheet, and is also clearly WILL'M SHAKSPERE, although from the tail of the letter *h* of the line above intervening between the *e* and *r*, Chalmers would fain raise an idle quibble as to the omission of a letter. The third signature has been the subject of greater controversy, and has usually been read, BY ME, WILLIAM SHAKSPEARE. Malone, however, was the first publicly to abjure this reading, and in his *Inquiry*, p. 117, owns the error to have been pointed out to him by an anonymous correspondent, who 'shewed most clearly, that the superfluous stroke in the letter *r* was only the tremor of his (Shakspere's) hand, and no *a*.' In this opinion, after the most scrupulous examination, I entirely concur. * * * * * * *

The next document is the mortgage deed, which was discovered in 1768 by Mr. Albany Wallis, a solicitor, among the title-deeds of the Rev. Mr. Featherstonehaugh, of Oxted, in Surrey, and was presented to Garrick. From the label of this, the fac-simile in Malone's edition of Shakspere, 1790, was executed, bearing this appearance, WM. SHAKSPE̅; and on this, in conjunction with the third signature of the will, was founded Malone's mistake in printing the name with an *a* in the second syllable. The deed was at that time in the possession of Mrs. Garrick; but in 1796, when Malone published his *Inquiry*, and had become convinced of his error, and of the fault of his engraver, in substituting what looks like the letter *a* instead of *re* (which it ought to be), the original document was missing, and could not be consulted for the purpose of rectifying the mistake. * *

The third document bearing Shakspere's signature, viz., the counterpart of the deed of bargain and sale, dated the day before the mortgage deed, was also found among Mr. Featherstonehaugh's Evidences, and in 1796 was in the hands of Mr. Wallis, who lent it to Mr. Malone to print in his often-quoted *Inquiry*. Here the signature is, beyond all cavil or suspicion, WILLIAM SHAKSPER, where the mark above is the usual abbreviation of the period for the final e.

The deed lost by Garrick is, as we have said, in the British Museum; the deed which Mr. Wallis lent to Malone is in the City of London Library, Guildhall.

With Sir F. Madden we adopt the view that all five signatures are alike, SHAKSPERE; yet Mr. Furnivall's conclusion is not justified. The actual case is familiar to the mathematician, in the guise of an urn containing a very large number of balls, of the colour of which we know nothing: from which a very small number of white balls are drawn. The number drawn being very small in comparison of the number in the urn, the drawing furnishes no ground whatever for the expectation that the urn contains more white balls than balls of any other *single* colour: still less, if possible, that the urn contains more white balls than balls that are non-white, *i. e.*, of *any* other colours. The fact is that such a drawing does not raise any probability as to the colour of the undrawn balls. Now, Shakespeare may very well have signed his name from 3,000 to 5,000 times in his life: and therefore the balls in the urn are very great in comparison of the number drawn, viz., five: and we cannot from such a drawing infer, even if 'Shakespeare knew how to spell his own name,' how he usually spelt it.

We must therefore fall back upon the style which (as Mr. Halliwell puts it) was bequeathed to us by Shakespeare's friends, was approved by himself in his two printed dedications to Lord Southampton, and which, with scarcely an exception, was adopted by his printers: viz., SHAKESPEARE.

CHAPTER II.

THE MEANING OF THE SURNAME.

DABBLERS in etymology are no worse than other dabblers in their conceit, presumption, and ignorance. How few among them have the least notion of the enormous mass of literature which deals with any one branch of the subject. In this single department of *Proper Names* there are books to be counted by hundreds in many European languages; and it is not too much to say that an explorer can as little afford to be ignorant of the leading works among them as the historian of Rome to ignore his Gibbon and his Niebuhr. In all likelihood, a glance at the analytical notice (far from perfect, however) of writers on the etymology and history of proper names, given by M. Noël in his Dictionary (Paris, 1806, pp. 93-97), would serve to scare away the most conceited of dabblers from the frontiers of so vast and perplexed a subject.

In this brief chapter we have no intention of meddling with it, beyond the ensuing brief notification. Eusebius Salverte, in his *History of Names*, vol. I, section xi, remarks:

The most natural way of distinguishing an individual, and the one which connects itself the most with the identity of name and person, is that of giving a name which shall remind others of his most striking peculiarities.* But this mode of naming is only adapted to a people who have hardly reached the lowest point in the [ascending] scale of civilisation, and who, being but one degree removed from the condition of the senseless savages who inhabit Bornou, are still, like them, destitute of any other system of nomenclature. When the community increases, and its general intercourse with other communities becomes more frequent, and more complicated within itself, there are soon too many members to be described as tall or short, dark or light, &c.; an allusion, therefore, to those features is not sufficiently distinctive. Remarkable deeds, occupations, tastes, habits, virtues, moral or physical defects, supply other names, which men are soon obliged to recognise and adopt.

This is our chief guiding light in theorizing on the origin of proper names: but induction has established a number of rules, which should be observed in such speculations. One of these is that we should primarily seek for the etymology of a man's surname in the language and among the customs and habits of the country to which he belongs; unless we possess evidence of his family having immigrated and become naturalized elsewhere.

Similarity of sound or of literal form, existing between a man's surname and certain words in his native language, is not a safe guide *per se:* though it may help us to a true inference in connection with biographical or historical details supporting it. There is not the least doubt that men were named from their exceptionable bodily characteristics, as well as from their avocations.

* From the English version of the Rev. L. H. Mordacque, 1862, vol. i, p. 58.

One class of surnames are indicative of a military extraction. The most remarkable of these, as illustrating the surname of our great bard, are

    Wagstaff,
    Wagspear,
    Shakeshaft,
    Shakelaunce,
    Breakspear,
  and Fewtarspear.

It is scarcely possible to resist the inference, that all these were intended to describe some warlike action: to *wag* or *shake* the *staff* or *shaft:* to *shake* the *launce*, to *break* or to *fewtar* the *spear*. To *fewtar* a spear, meant to place it in the rest. A correspondent in *Notes and Queries* (5th S. ii. 2), Mr. C. W. Bardsley, calls attention to the occurrence of four of these names: viz., 'Robert Waggestaff,' in Proc. and Ord. Privy Council (indeed this name and Shakeshaft have living representatives), 'Mabill Wag-spere' in the Coldingham Priory Records (Surtees Society), 'Henry Shake-launce' in the Hundred Rolls, 'Hugh Shake-shaft' in St. Ann's Register, Manchester (date 1744); and he also adds, 'William Shakespere' in Bury St. Edmunds Wills (Camden Society). Nicholas Breakspear is a notorious example of the fifth name on our list; and the last, which is obsolete, was once an ordinary surname.

Dr. Charnock, in *Notes and Queries* (5th S. ii. 405), ventured to assert, upon his own unsupported authority, that *Wagstaff* and *Fewtarspear* were local names. Whether or not any case can be made out for Wagstaff, it is almost certain that Fewtarspear was not taken from a place, but was the name of one who fewtar's the spear: and Rev. W. W. Skeat, in *Notes and Queries* (5th S. ii. 444) quoted from Spenser's *Faery Queen* (iv. 5-45) the line,

> His *speare* he *feutred*, and at him it bore.

Mr. W. J. Bernhard Smith, in *Notes and Queries* (5th S. ii. 484), quoted four examples of the expression to *feutre the spear* from *La Mort d'Arthure*, vol. ii. c. 94, 95, 98.

'Then was King Marke ashamed, and therewith he *feutred* his *speare*, and ran against Sir Trian.'

'That saw Sir Dinadan, and hee *feutred* his *speare*, and ranne to one of Sir Berluse's fellowes.'

'And then they *feutred* their *speares*, and this Knight came so egerly that he smote downe Sir Ewane alone.'

'So Sir Agrawaine *feutred* his *speare*, and that other was ready, and smote him downe over his horse taile to the earth.'

Nothing could be more complete than the parallel between these two names—*Fewtarspeare* and *Shakespeare*. The heavy speare was used in tilting, and was *feutred** before the onset: the light speare, or lance, was brandished or *shaken*, before being hurled. The derivation of these names from the warlike acts described is simple and natural; and is confirmed by many other surnames, descriptive of distinguishing actions. Just as Armstrong and Strongitharm express the strength of arm of the warrior, armourer, or smith, so do Fewtarspeare,

---

* Does this word mean laid in a rest made of *felt*; or does it mean *fettled*, *i. e.*, made ready, set in order? We leave the philologers to decide the point. It can hardly be related to *fewterer*, a hound-keeper.

and Shakespeare, indicate the military calling of the ancestor who first bore the name.

Dr. R. S. Charnock and Dr. Charles Mackay will not allow that the name of our bard originated in this manner. Dr. Charnock puts forward two totally inconsistent derivations, on an equality with which he puts a conjecture occurring previously in *Notes and Queries:* Dr. Mackay, in *The Athenæum*, confidently proposes a fourth; and another correspondent of *Notes and Queries* a fifth. Here is the wonderful pentad.

French	Jacques Pierre (or Jakespear).
Saxon	Sigisbert.
German	Schachs-burh (or Isaacsbury).
Celtic	Schaespeir (*i. e.*, Drylegs).
Florentine	Lapus Biragus (or Jacobsbire).

I.—Jacques Pierre.

SHAKSPEARE, Derivation of. The name, Shakspeare, no doubt originated in the Norman or French edition of the double-beloved disciple name (Jacques-Pierre, James-Peter, Jakespear) of which it is composed; the initial J being pronounced *sh*, as in many other instances, viz.:

Shenkins	for Jenkins.
Sherard	— Gerard.
Shiles	— Giles.
Sherry	— Jerry.
Sheridan	— Jeridan (Old Jerry).
Shenstone	— Johnstone (Johnson).
She	— Je, in Switzerland, and elsewhere where the French language is provincialised, &c.

With such a self-evident derivation before us, we may therefore dispense with the unlikely reference to the shaking of a spear, which most probably had nothing to do with the origin of the name when first invented, being only a suggestion from its accidental English form; though the idea once started, the name may with some have seemed to be recommended by it.

Those who consider that Shakspeare originated in spear-shaking rely on 'Breakspear,' 'Winspear,' &c., as analogous, these names having a like termination in, and apparent reference to, action with a spear; but this illustration is of the kind *ignotum per ignotius*. We do not know enough of Breakspeare, &c., to justify us in saying that their origin was connected with spears; nor applying any inferences from them to other names. Probably Breakspear (a priest) was in part named after St. Peter, the chief of the apostles, and not after spears. Winspear almost looks like 'Owen' or (John?) 'Peter.'—R. T. A.—*Notes and Queries*, 2nd S. xi. 86. (See also 4th S. x. 516 and xi. 133.)

II.—Sigisbert.

We now have little difficulty in tracing the name 'Shakespere,' which I take to be no other than a corruption of SIGISBERT, 'renowned for victory' (from Old German *sieg*, Anglo-Saxon *sige*, Franc. et Alam *sigo*, 'victory'); thus Sigisbert, Sigsbert, Sigsber, Siksper, Shiksper, Shaksper, SHAKSPERE. I do not find the name Sigisbert, but there is Sigibert (whence very many English names have been corrupted) and Sigismerus, as well as Segimerus and Sigimar, and also Sigismund, whence by contraction the Italian form Sismondi. If it should be advanced that we have the name 'Wagstaff,' I answer that the last syllable in that and in many other personal names [this must mean, *which also occurs* in many other personal names] has nothing whatever to do with a 'staff,' which I can prove if necessary.—Dr. R. S. Charnock.—*Notes and Queries*, 2nd S. ix. 459.*

---

* In *Notes and Queries* (2nd S. x. 15) Mr. R. Ferguson points out (1) that *Sigisbert* might produce *Sicisper*, on known etymological analogues; but Sicisper could hardly produce Shakspere; (2) that the surname *Shakeshaft* (taking the place of the disqualified Wagstaff) is still an obstacle to Dr. Charnock's doctrine. To this Dr. Charnock rejoins that he will not allow the *shaft*, any more than the *staff*, to mean what it appears to mean. It is either *haft*, or *haved*, or something else: but not our *shaft*. *Staff*, he asserts, is *sted*.

III.—Shachs-burh (Isaacsbury).

The most reasonable derivation of 'Shakspeare' is that from *Jacques Pierre*; but the name would corrupt from *Shachs-burh*. The German surname Schach would seem to be a corruption of Isaac. Conf. Sach, Sacchi, from Isaac; Sachs, Sax, from Isaacs. I suppose we may now expect a new pamphlet, 'Was the divine Williams of Jewish descent?'

Dr. R. S. Charnock.—*Notes and Queries* (5th S. ii. 405).*

---

* From the concluding sentence one might infer that Dr. Charnock was, all through, poking fun at us: for who, except the all-too-learned Doctor himself, would be likely to advocate the Jewish descent of our great bard—who but the discoverer of this Jewish etymology? However, on the whole, we are bound to give him credit for being in earnest: so that we are led to the following conclusions:

1. That Dr. Charnock believes *Shakspere* to be a corruption of *Sigisbert*.
2. That Dr. Charnock believes *Shakspeare* may have corrupted from *Shachs-burh*, which he believes to be identical with *Isaacsbury*.
3. That Dr. Charnock — holding both these views — believes (nevertheless and notwithstanding) that *Jacques Pierre* is 'the most reasonable derivation.'

The Rev. Walter W. Skeat remarks:

I do not see why English etymology should be considered a fit subject for such unintelligent guess work.—*Notes and Queries*, 5th S. ii. 444.

We do. It is good for Messrs. Skeat, Morris, Ellis, and all other philologers to see, in an extreme case, how utterly foolish is learning without common sense. Indeed Mr. Skeat assents: for he subsequently remarks, of Mr. Sala's speculations on *Shambles*, 'I think his remarks are extremely valuable, as showing how much it is still the fashion, in questions of English etymology * * * to disregard entirely not only the history of the words we use, but also the history of the sounds composing those words.'—*Notes and Queries*, 5th S. v. 261.

IV.—Schacspeir (Dryshanks).

Mid-England, where Shakespeare was born and bred, was not so thoroughly Saxonised, either in speech or blood, as the southern and eastern shores of the island. The river Avon has a Gaelic or British name. The Forest of Arden, where he chased the deer, means in Celtic the 'high' forest. His mother's name was Celtic, if not his father's; for it is possible and probable that Shakespeare is but a Saxonised corruption of the Celtic Schacspeir, or Chaksper, as his father wrote it,* which signifies—*shac*, or *seac*, dry: and *speir* shanks, as we have in our day the Saxon names of Sheepshank and Cruikshank, suggested by a personal malformation or deformity, in days when surnames were not common, and applied as a nickname to some early ancestor of the family. Not alone Shakespeare, but Spencer, Ben Jonson, Marlow, and other writers of that time employed British words, which were then well understood by the common people, but which have not been explained by modern commentators, for the sufficient reason that they have never looked for the explanations in the only place where it is possible to find them—the language of the unexterminated Britons, and of the Anglo-Saxon sons of British mothers, who retained in after-life the homely words of the nursery and the workshop. * * * * * * —Dr. Charles Mackay.—*The Athenæum*, 2nd October, 1875, p. 437.

V.—Schacobspire.

For myself, however, I cling to the hope that our bard's family came from Italy, and that his surname is a corruption of that of the well-known Florentine historian, Lapus Biragus. It is an undoubted fact that Lapus is the Florentine abbreviation of Jacob, or Jacobs; so that the Anglicised form of his name would be *Jacobsbirage*, or *Jacobsbire* [? Jacobsbirg], or *Schacobspire*, whence *Shakspere* would very naturally corrupt. I wonder Dr. Charnock missed this.—Jabez.—*Notes and Queries*, 5th S. v. 352.

---

* John Shakespeare apparently could not sign his name. He is only known to us as a marksman.

Even if we allow that Dr. Charnock was not poking fun at us, we cannot as readily suppose the last correspondent to be in earnest, but rather incline to the belief, that by perpetrating an excess of philological absurdity, he is bent on throwing deserved ridicule on the speculation of his predecessor, whose sole object was, apparently, to discredit the simplest and most probable derivation of our bard's surname.

CHAPTER III.

SHAKESPEARE'S TRADITIONAL BIRTHDAY.*

THE birth of Shakespeare is, I believe, universally celebrated on the 23rd April. The tradition on which the celebrants rely is, that he was born on the 23rd April, 1564, Old Style ; and it is somewhat discomforting to precisians to learn that in Shakespeare's day the New Style (which was not then observed in England) was ten days in advance of the Old ; and that there is now a difference of twelve days between them : so that the 23rd April, O.S., was in 1564 the 3rd May, N.S. ; a date which at the present time corresponds to the 5th May, N.S. It has accordingly been made a question whether we should not celebrate the occasion on either the 3rd or the 5th May, in every year.

I refer to this question, which springs out of the difference of Style, not for the purpose of attempting to settle it, but simply because it has been so often asserted that Shakespeare

* From the Transactions of the Royal Society of Literature, vol. x. New Series. Read, May 17, 1871.

and Cervantes died on the same day : the fact being that Shakespeare survived Cervantes ten days.

It is even more discomforting to the punctual keeper of birthdays to find that the tradition of Shakespeare's birth on the 23rd April, 1564, O.S., cannot be traced to any authentic source. The student of Shakespeare-biography soon becomes inured to scepticism. One cherished fact after another falls before the scythe of criticism, till only a small and unimportant residue remains. In sheer despair of ascertaining facts, the majority of biographers have been content to weave a tissue of fictions. The most trustworthy memoirs of the bard are those which support the meagre text by a formidable array of foot-notes, adduced in disproof of nearly everything that forms the very staple of the old biographies.

Such work is like pulling down a National Gallery to make room for a peep-show. There is, indeed, some little proof of Shakespeare's lineage; and he himself seems to have been born in the year 1564 at the traditional birthplace. But having launched our hero on that 'sea of troubles' which every mortal has to navigate as best he may—some to reach the wished-for haven, some, on shoal or quicksand, like the headstrong man in Æschylus, to perish unwept, unknown (ἄκλαυστος, ἄιστος)—we lose sight of the poet to obtain a few partial and isolated glimpses of his outer life: but in the hands of biographers, these glimpses become the more shining parts of 'a round *and* varnished tale.' I, too, can find pleasure in the creations of a semi-prophetic ingenuity; but I cannot treat those creations as historical facts.

> Sunt et mihi carmina ; me quoque dicunt
> Vatem pastores ; sed non ego credulus illis.

It would occupy too much time and paper if I were to sift, in detail, the traditional life of Shakespeare : but I may at least indicate a few points, besides that of the birthday, which are repeated by almost every biographer, and which have hitherto remained unsupported by any satisfactory evidence.

1. We are told that Shakespeare 'had been in his younger yeares a schoolmaster in the country.' We get that scrap of news from conscientious John Aubrey, whose manuscript (circa 1680) is in the Ashmolean collection ; and Aubrey says he got it 'from Mr. Beeston.' This was probably William Beeston, Governor of 'the King and Queen's young Company of Players,' who lost his office in 1640, and was then succeeded by D'Avenant.

2. We are told further that Shakespeare had been formerly 'bound apprentice to a butcher' in Stratford, but 'run from his master to London.' We get that from a letter dated the 10th April, 1693, written by a Mr. John Dowdall to a Mr. Edward Southwell. Who they were we do not know : but we know that this Mr. Dowdall professed to have obtained it from the Parish Clerk of Stratford, who was at that time over eighty years of age. His testimony, after all, was, probably, but ill-remembered gossip.

3. We are further told that, in all likelihood, Shakespeare had been to school ; but we have no evidence whatever of the fact. Mr. J. O. Halliwell (Phillipps), in his *Life of Shakespeare*, 1848, p. 92, makes no question of Shakespeare having

been educated at the Stratford Grammar School, and naïvely remarks :

> It would be a very difficult task to identify the exact position of the room in which Shakespeare was educated.

But it would not be a whit more difficult to identify the exact position in that room of the form on which Shakespeare sat! It is all one, surely, since we really do not know that he ever attended that school, or any other. If he did go to school, I make no doubt that, according to the estimate of the day, he was accounted a shocking dunce; that many a time and oft he felt the remorseless 'bob' of the village pedagogue, and took his stand on a stool in the corner of the school-room, wearing the ensign of duncedom on his head. If, as Mr. Harness fancifully conjectures, he was lame, he may have contracted his lameness through the caning of his master or the tunding of his elders in the school! Be that as it may, we may be quite sure that he suffered, if not for his pains, at least for his brains; just as, at a later period, Goldsmith and Byron were punished as incurable dunces, and the immortal Gauss was flogged for his audacity in solving an arithmetical problem before the rest of the school had taken it down. It is pleasant to indulge in such picturesque imaginings: but imagination is not biography.

4. As to another tradition in Shakespeare's life, viz., the deer-stealing episode, I am disposed, with De Quincey, to discredit it altogether, and even to treat it as a myth invented to account for Shakespeare's seeming animosity toward Sir Thomas Lucy. My late lamented friend, Charles Holte

Bracebridge, following the lead of Malone, has apparently settled the question, and proved that Charlecote Park was *not* a deer preserve,* and that to have sported at Fulbroke would *not* have been a breach of the law. The tale, after all, rests on a manuscript of the Rev. William Fulman, who died in 1688. Fulman having bequeathed it to the Rev. Richard Davies, and died, that gentleman recorded the story on the manuscript in his own handwriting. Mr. Davies died in 1708; and the manuscript is now in Corpus Christi College, Oxford. Whence he obtained the story he does not tell us.

5. Lastly, we are told that when Shakespeare did get to London, he earned a livelihood by holding horses at the doors of the theatres. I fear that is a myth too. We get the story from the anonymous author of *The Lives of the Poets of Great Britain and Ireland*, 1753, and he says he obtained it from a gentleman whose name he does not give.† But after these two anonyms we get on a little better: for anonym the second is said to have heard it from Dr. Newton; and it is further said that Newton got it from Pope; and that Pope got it from Rowe; and that Rowe got it—with a mass of similar rubbish—from Betterton, the actor; and that Betterton got it

---

* Since writing this, Mr. J. O. Phillipps has called my attention to a curious entry in *The Egerton Papers*, 4to, 1840, p. 355, where, among the 'List of Presents at Harefield,' in the year 44 Elizabeth, we read:

vj^s viij^d Bucke, j . . . . Sir Tho. Lucie.

taking that for what it is worth, it fails to disprove Mr. Bracebridge's conclusion.

† Said by some to have been Dr. Johnson, because Shiels, who wrote the greater part of the *Lives* for Cibber, was Dr. Johnson's amanuensis.

from Sir William D'Avenant: but there we lose the scent. Of such hearsays is our life of Shakespeare manufactured.

After this somewhat long exordium, I turn to the principal subject of this paper. Our authorities for the dates of Shakespeare's birth and death are these: (1) the register of his baptism; (2) the register of his burial; (3) the inscription on the tablet under his bust in the chancel of Stratford Church; (4) some manuscript notes of Oldys' on Langbaine's *Account of the English Dramatic Poets*, 1691; and (5) manuscript notes by the Rev. Joseph Greene, master of the Grammar School at Stratford, and some extracts from the Stratford register. I give exact copies of all these.

1.—Extract from Register of Baptisms at Stratford Church:

   1564
   April
   26 Gulielmus filius Johannes Shakspere.

2.—Extract from Register of Burials at Stratford Church:

   1616
   April
   25 Will Shakspere, Gent.

3.—Inscription on the tablet under Shakespeare's bust (in the lower right-hand corner):

   OBIIT ANO DO¹ 1616
   ÆTATIS, 53. DIE 23 AP.

4.—Certain manuscript notes on Langbaine (1691), by Oldys (in the British Museum):

See the sculpture and Inscription in Dugdale's Warwickshire.	Obiit An. Dom. 1616
	             53
	Æt. 53. die 23 Apr. 1563
	   * * * *

> I have now no more to do, but to close up all, with an account of his Death; which was on the
> (¹ 23rd of April, 1616.*

5.—Manuscript notes, in the handwriting of Rev. Joseph Greene, on some extracts from the Stratford Register:

> 'Died at the age of 53' (on the burial item, as in 2).
> 'Born April 23, 1564' (on the baptismal item, as in 1).

Boswell, the son of Johnson's biographer, who completed Malone's life of Shakespeare, doubtless had most of these materials before him when he drew the following inference:

> He died on his birthday, April 23rd, 1616, and had exactly completed his fifty-second year.

But this is not in strict accord with the authorities. If we accept the testimony of the insculpture, we need not disallow that of Greene's second note. That Shakespeare was born on or before the 26th April, 1564, we must allow; for he was baptized on that day; and we can only bring the insculpture into disagreement with the tradition by supposing that Shakespeare was born on the 24th, the 25th, or the 26th: then, indeed, he would have been still in his fifty-second year when he died.

The use which has been made of Oldys' notes is a curious

---

* The black ink represents Langbaine's text, the red letter Oldys' notes and lines. The mark opposite the last underwritten line may be the figure 2 or the letter Q. I think it is the latter, and that its function is to express his doubt as to the relative date.

and instructive example of the untrustworthiness of critics. As far as my search has extended, all the biographers who cite Oldys do not fairly represent him. The late Mr. Bolton Corney remarks:

> Oldys had much experience in biographic composition; but he asserts that Shakespeare was born on the 23rd April, 1563, and that he died at the age of 53, A.D. 1616. He converts the day and month of the decease of Shakespeare into the day and month of his birth; contradicts the parish register as to the year of his birth; and contradicts the monumental inscription as to his age at the time of his decease. The assertions of Oldys as testified by his handwriting, have no other basis than his own misconceptions.—*Notes and Queries*, 3rd S., v. 225.

It is a fact that in his manuscript notes for a life of Shakespeare (written on the margins of the Museum copy of *Langbaine*) Oldys assigns April 23, 1563, as the day of Shakespeare's birth, a mistake which evidently arose from his subtraction of 53 from 1616: but he certainly had some doubt on the subject: for he queries the asserted day of Shakespeare's death. Oldys' method of finding the year of his birth is admissible only on the assumption that he knew that Shakespeare was born on one of the three days intervening between the 23rd and the 27th April. If any inference is to be drawn from Oldys' first note, it must be based on the assumption that, by the subtraction of 53 from 1616, he was observing an unexceptionable method, and in that case the inference would be that Shakespeare was believed by him to have been born on the 24th or 25th, or even possibly on the day of his baptism, the 26th April. Clearly he could not have been born later in the month: and if he were born as early as the 23rd April, *in the year* 1563, he would have entered his 54th year when he died; just as he must have been born on or before the 23rd April, in the year 1564, in order that his death might take place in his 53rd year. It is plain to us that Oldys did not clearly perceive these simple arithmetical relations: and I dare say they have puzzled many other educated persons. Anyhow, Mr. Corney must have failed to see his way through these various details of date, or he would not have categorically committed himself to the so-called *Argument on the assumed birthday of Shakespeare.**

Mr. Bolton Corney's argument is thus epitomized by himself:

As Shakespeare died on the 23rd April [1616], in his fifty-*third* year, he must have been born *before the* 23rd *April*, 1564.

This happens to be just one of those precise categorical assertions which admits of exact refutation. It is false in the same sense in which any arithmetical calculation is false. For instance, if it were demanded of me how many days elapse between the first and last days of January, and I should answer, 'there *must be* less than thirty days,' I am asserting a necessity which follows from something in my thoughts, and

---

* Mr. Corney's *Argument* was in 1864 'reduced to shape' in a pamphlet of 16 pp.; where he writes, 'So Master Oldys, in some non-lucid moment, underscores *die* 23 *Apr.*—subtracts 53 from 1616—and writes down 1563. He assumes that the words *anno ætatis* 53 are equivalent to *vixit annos* 53, and that the words *die* 23 *Aprilis* refer to *anno ætatis*, instead of being the object of *Obiit*. Such is the process, *never before described*, by which the birthday of Shakspere was discovered.'—Mr. Corney's Tract, p. 7.

not from the mere terms of the question. That assertion is therefore false. Mr. Bolton Corney's assertion is just as false.

It is also as *demonstrably* false: and herein lies the only difficulty with which I have to contend in this refutation. I am sorry to say, that, according to my experience, the general mind is averse from demonstration. If a conclusion rest on probable evidence, or on feeling only, and people are invited to entertain it, and exhorted to embrace it, there are reasonable hopes that it will find many adherents, upon whose minds it has wrought to the extent of producing an impression in its favour, which I cannot describe as either belief or faith without doing violence to philosophical language. But if, on the contrary, the conclusion advanced be supported by an iron chain of demonstration, the general mind, either grudging the exertion of thought necessary to master the proof, or flying off under the influence of anger from what seems an *invasion of its freedom, a restriction on its maundering habits*, will not away with it.*

---

* This position was curiously, and to me very interestingly, exemplified on an occasion when I had to show the rotation of the moon on her axis, in opposition to the crotchet of the late Mr. Jellinger Symons. I reduced my premises to machinery, and exhibited the conclusion by the motion of its parts. I had a model of the earth, into which (merely for convenience) I had inserted an iron rod, to which a ball, representing the moon, was attached. When the latter was made to circulate around the former, the former exhibited the phenomenon (admitted by both parties to the controversy) of one unvarying hemisphere of the moon being constantly presented to the earth. But, firmly fixed on the spindle or axis of the moon (which was perpendicular to the iron rod, and worked freely in it), was also a disc divided at the edge into degrees and numbered, and an

The simple denial, or contradictory, of Mr. Corney's assertion is this:

> If Shakespere died on the 23rd April [1616], in his fifty-third year, he may have been born on the 23rd April, 1564.

This is the proposition I undertake to establish.

But before doing so, I wish it to be understood that by the assumption of the most unquestionable premises I can prove the direct opposite, or contrary, of Mr. Corney's assertion, viz.:

> If Shakespeare was born on the 23rd April [1564], he must have entered his fifty-third year on the 23rd April, 1616.

Let me consider this point first.

A pretty extensive adduction of authorities on the question, 'When does a person complete the first, second, third, etc., year of his age?' justifies me in the statement that the late Professor De Morgan was the only writer (save, perhaps, Mr. Corney) who ever asserted that the duration of a year is prolonged beyond the vigil of its anniversary. In an article

index, or pointer, with an arrow head, was inserted into the side of the moon, and thus pointed out the angular amount by which the relative positions of the moon and the disc might be changed. By means of an unnecessary mechanical contrivance, for which I might very well have substituted a weight, this disc was kept constantly in one position with respect to the frame of the machine. By turning a handle the moon was made to revolve, and the index showed the revolution of the moon on the spindle. 'This motion is either real or apparent; if it be apparent, it must be the disc which revolves on the moon's axis. But we have "ocular demonstration" that the disc does not so revolve.' There was not, I am certain, a single person in the lecture-room who did not feel, in some degree, the rigour of the proof; and I shall never forget the howl of indignation with which this was greeted. The great majority showed me, in a most unmistakable manner, that such an interference with their liberty of mind was not to be tolerated for an instant.

contributed to the *Companion to the Almanac*, 1850, the learned professor wrote :

> The anniversary of birth used to be celebrated as the first day of a new year ; it is now considered as the completion of an old one.

To this Mr. A. E. Brae, in his very able work, *An Examination of the Century Question*, 1850 (p. 25), replied :

> To assert, however, that in this respect moderns differ from the ancients, is a libel upon moderns which they certainly do not deserve. There is no difference in respect of birthday usage. It is with moderns, as it was with ancients, the celebration of *renewed birth ;* and the very meaning of the expression 'New Year's Day,' the anniversary of the year, is of itself sufficient to show that Mr. De Morgan's *modern instances* are as incorrect as his ancient inferences.

This seems to me to be undoubtedly correct. Yet, even adopting Professor De Morgan's view, the usage of the sixteenth and seventeenth centuries would decidedly place Shakespeare in his 53rd year on the day of his death, supposing it to have been also the 52nd anniversary of his birth, or, counting the birth itself as one, the 53rd event.*

---

* According to the probabilities of the case, an innumerable number of persons would be found to have died on the anniversary of birth, and it is, therefore, not surprising that a considerable number of eminent persons are known to have done so. John Williams, Archbishop of York, died on his birthday, March 25th, in the 69th year of his age : '*anno ætatis* 68° *expleto.*' *Hacket's Life of Archbishop Williams*, 1693, fo. p. 229. He was born March 25th, in 1582, and therefore died on March 25th, 1650. Archdeacon Sandford (of Coventry) died on his birthday, March 22nd, in the 73rd year of his age ; and as he was born March 22nd, 1801, he must have died on March 22nd, 1873. The first Sir Henry Holland died on his birthday, October 27th, in the 87th year of his age. He was born October 27th, 1787 ; and therefore died October 27th, 1873. These examples sufficiently illustrate our position, though many more might readily be adduced.

The fact that on every anniversary of a birth a new year has already been entered upon, is evident in the very attempt to deny it; for, otherwise, in the *first year* there would be two birthdays, the real one and its anniversary. In order that every year may have its new year's day—*i. e.*, that the first year may have its birthday, and every succeeding year its anniversary, that anniversary, or new year's day, must be the first day of each year. Accordingly, it is quite unquestionable that, supposing Shakespeare to have been born on the 23rd April, 1564, he was already in his fifty-third year at any time on the 23rd April, 1616. This proof is indeed *sans réplique*, unless we allow a division of days. I am not aware of Mr. Corney having taken refuge in the doctrine that in the inscription on Shakespeare's tomb, the day mentioned is not a unit, but a number (as twenty-four hours) susceptible of division, one part of which might be counted in one year, and the other part in another. But as this is the only resource left to any one attempting the refutation of my position, I will now address myself to that point.

If the critical exactness of determining such fractions of days be attempted, it must take into its account the fraction by which the year exceeds 365 days; for by so much must the hour of birth be advanced in each succeeding year, and retrenched again in leap year. The practical effect of this would be that no two birth-epochs would harmonize, and a calculation, something like that of a horoscope, would have to be entered into for every successive anniversary of birth! Need I add, that there is not a particle of evidence on record that such critical exactness in determining births was ever attempted except for astrological purposes.

The establishment of the contrary position,

> If Shakespeare was born on the 23rd April, 1564, he must have entered his fifty-third year on the 23rd April, 1616,

logically includes the contradictory of Mr. Corney's thesis. But in order to establish that contradictory independently of the narrower proposition, it is only requisite to exhibit one or more alternatives to the position which he asserts as a necessary inference, *i. e.*, to show that in certain cases,

> If Shakespeare died on the 23rd April, 1616, in his fifty-third year, he may have been born on the 23rd April, 1564.

The following are three of such alternatives:

I. If the writer of the inscription on the tomb adopted the usage of his nation and his time, counting the anniversary of Shakespeare's birth as the first day of a new year—disallowing fractions of days.

II. If he did so—yet allowed a division of the day, and knew that Shakespeare's birth took place in the earlier and his death in the later portion of the day.

III. If the inscription, though good evidence for the date of Shakespeare's death, is not (in the absence of an exact date) to be regarded as good evidence for the date of his birth—a view by no means absurd, since the term *year of age* (*ætate suâ*) is open to such uncertain interpretation, and so often the record of mere guesswork or repute.

In any one of these cases we may accept both the

traditional birthday of Shakespeare and the day of his death as recorded on the monumental tablet. Mr. Bolton Corney's argument would require that each of these cases should be severally disallowed. He simply ignored them all! *

* These strictures on Mr. Corney's pamphlet were written in his lifetime, and intended to invite his counter-criticism. He died September 10, 1870, after this paper was promised. As printed in the *Transactions* of the Royal Society of Literature, it contains some passages unjustly taxing Mr. Corney with inaccuracy in quoting Oldys' notes. I was misled by the collation of a friend in the Manuscript Department of the British Museum, who strangely overlooked some of the notes of *Oldys*.

POSTSCRIPT ON CERTAIN ANNOTATED COPIES OF LANGBAINE.

THE following valuable note is from *Notes and Queries*, 3rd Series, Feb. 1, 1862, pp. 82-83.

"The most valuable and curious work left by Oldys is an annotated copy of Gerard Langbaine's *Account of the Early Dramatick Poets*, Oxford, 1691, 8vo. It has already been stated (*ante*, p. 3), that the first *copy* of this work with his notes had passed into the hands of Mr. Coxeter. After Mr. Coxeter's death his books and manuscripts were purchased by Osborne, and were offered for sale in 1748. The book in question, No. 10,131 in Osborne's Catalogue for that year, was purchased either by Theophilus Cibber, or by some bookseller who afterwards put it into his hands; and from the notes of Oldys and Coxeter, the principal part of the additional matter furnished by Cibber (or rather by Shiels) for the *Lives of the Poets*, five vols. 12mo, 1753, was unquestionably derived. Mr. Coxeter's manuscripts are mentioned in the title-page, to whom, therefore, the exclusive credit of the work is assigned, but which really belongs as much, if not more, to Oldys.

Oldys purchased a *second* Langbaine in 1727, and continued to annotate it till the latest period of his life. This copy was purchased by Dr. Birch, who bequeathed it to the British Museum. [Press Mark, C. 28, g. 1.] It is not interleaved, but filled with notes written in the margins and between the lines in an extremely small hand. Birch granted the loan of it to Dr. Percy, Bishop of Dromore, who made a transcript of the notes into an interleaved copy of Langbaine in four vols. 8vo. It was from Bishop Percy's copy that Mr. Joseph Haslewood annotated his Langbaine. He says, 'His Lordship was so kind as to favour me with the loan of this book, with a generous permission to make what use of it I might think proper; and when he went to Ireland, he left it with Mr. Nichols, for the benefit of the new edition of the *Tatler*, *Spectator*, and *Guardian*, with Notes and Illustrations, to which work his Lordship was by his other valuable communications a very beneficial contributor.'

George Steevens likewise made a transcript of Oldys's notes into a copy of Langbaine, which at the sale of his library in 1800, was purchased by

Richardson, the bookseller, for £9, who resold it to Sir S. Egerton Brydges in the same year for fourteen guineas. At the sale of the Lee Priory Library in 1834, it fell into the hands of Thorpe, of Bedford Street, Covent Garden, from whom the late Dr. Bliss purchased it on February 7, 1835, for nine guineas. It is now in the British Museum.

Malone, Isaac Reed, and the Rev. Rogers Ruding, also made transcripts of Oldys's notes. The Malone transcript is now at Oxford; but Ruding's has not been traced. In a cutting from one of Thorpe's catalogues, preserved by Dr. Bliss, it is stated to be in two volumes, the price £5. 5s.; that Ruding transcribed them in 1784, and that his additions are very numerous. In Heber's Catalogue (part iv, No. 1215) is another copy of Langbaine, with very important additions by Oldys, Steevens, and Reed. This was purchased by Rodd for £4. 4s. In 1845, Edward Vernon Utterson had an interleaved Langbaine. What became of it?"

It is more important to inquire what has become of the copy of Langbaine first annotated by Oldys. After making various inquiries in London and Oxford, I am still unable to trace it.—C. M. I.

CHAPTER IV.

THE AUTHORSHIP OF THE WORKS ATTRIBUTED TO SHAKESPEARE.*

ONE does not look for popularity in the attempt to disturb a popular belief. One may, nevertheless, bespeak a favourable consideration for the most startling views, if only they are supported by facts, and their advocacy is addressed to a competent tribunal.

An American essayist, who speaks from an intellectual eminence which justifies the speculation, asserts—

that what is best written or done by genius, in the world, was no man's work, but came by wide social labour, when a thousand wrought like one, sharing the same impulse.†

He points to the English Bible, the Anglican Ritual, and the Dramas of Shakespeare, as examples in point. He remembers, and so must we, that Shakespeare did not write for fame;

---

* From the Transactions of the Royal Society of Literature, Vol. IX, new series. Read, January 22, 1868.

† *Representative Men*, by R. W. Emerson. A like passage occurs in his masterly Essay on Compensation, *Essays*, 1841, p. 108.

that he claimed no property in his published works, and did not assert their originality. If their whole merit has been assigned to him, it was by no act of his. They were produced for representation, not for literature, and their producer was rather a showman than an author.

The time may come when every personal interest about the man will be forgotten, when the schoolboys of an American empire will confound the man with his works, as schoolboys nowadays are said sometimes to look upon Euclid as the name of a science. When that time comes, the reading public will be no more astonished by the assertion that Lord Bacon wrote Shakespeare than we are by the assertion that Babrius wrote Æsop. But at present we have not wholly identified Shakespeare with 'his booke;' and when Lady Bab, in Garrick's farce, *High Life below Stairs*, asks 'Did you never read Shikspur?' and Mrs. Kitty replies, 'Shikspur? Shikspur? Who wrote it?' the humour is still as fresh as the day when it was written.

Before seriously entertaining Lady Bab's question, we must determine in what sense it is to be understood. If the inquiry be after some one man who originated, designed, and executed the various dramas of the 'booke,' let us consider whether such a requirement would be reasonable in the case of any great work of art. Was Tennyson the sole author of those Arthurian Romances which have won for him a corner of Spenser's footstool? Not at all. The legends and materials were made to his hand. Yet, in the truest sense, Tennyson may be called the author of the *Idylls of the King*, for he re-imagined and re-created them, without infringing the rights of another. In this sense, then, was the actor, William Shakespeare, the author of *The Merry Wives of Windsor, The Taming of the Shrew, The Life and Death of King John, The Life of King Henry V, the First, Second, and Third Parts of King Henry VI, The Life of King Henry VIII, Titus Andronicus, Romeo and Juliet, Timon of Athens, Hamlet, and Pericles?* It seems not. You may suppose I have not selected those thirteen plays at random. The fact is, that not one of them is free from the suspicion that another hand has contributed to that fame which has been appropriated to Shakespeare alone.

We are here introduced into the thick of some of the most intricate problems of dramatic criticism, which I can only glance at now. Among the waifs which the wreck of the early Elizabethan drama has bequeathed to us are four plays bearing the following names: *The Troublesome Reigne of John, King of England,* 4to, 1591, 1611, 1622; *The First Part of the Contention betwixt the Two Famous Houses of Yorke and Lancaster,* small 8vo, 1594, and 4to, 1600 and 1619; *The True Tragedie of Richard, Duke of Yorke,* 4to, 1595, 1600, and 1619; and *A Pleasant Conceited Historie called the Taming of a Shrew,* 4to, 1594, 1596, and 1607.

These respectively correspond to four of the plays attributed to Shakespeare, viz., *The Life and Death of King John,* the *Second and Third Parts of King Henry VI,* and *The Taming of the Shrew.*

It is nearly certain that Shakespeare did not write a line of the old *King John,* on which he constructed *his* play so named.

It is equally certain that he had no hand whatever in the old *Taming of a Shrew*, which we have every reason for believing to have been written by Christopher Marlow; but, on the other hand, it would be a rash inference that Shakespeare had used this play in the composition of his own. Some day the knot, perhaps, will be untied; and then we shall probably see Charles Knight's conjecture established by the discovery of evidence that Marlow and Shakespeare used one and the same original in the composition of their dramas. I wish it were possible for us to see our way as clearly in dealing with *The First Part of the Contention* and *The True Tragedie.* They *seem* to have been originally the joint compositions of Marlow and Robert Greene, not improbably touched by Shakespeare subsequently, and exhibiting those touches in the edition of 1619; anyhow, Marlow's hand is unmistakably apparent in both plays. The following examples are adduced in support of this view by Mr. Halliwell in his edition of the *First Sketches of the Second and Third Parts of Henry VI*, printed for the Shakespeare Society, 1843:

The wild O'Neile, my lord, is up in arms, With troupes of Irish kernes, that uncontroul'd Do plant themselves within the English pale. *First Part of the Contention.*	The wild O'Neile, with swarms of Irish kernes, Lives uncontroul'd within the English pale. Marlow's *Edward II.*
This villain, being but captain of a pinnace, threatens more plagues	I remember, Ismena, that Epicurus measured every man's dyet by

than Abradas, the great Macedonian pirate.—*Ibid.*	his own principles, and Abradas, the great Macedonian pirat, thought every one had a letter of mart that bare sayles in the ocean. Green's *Penelope's Web*, 1588.
What, will the aspiring blood of Lancaster Sink into the ground? I thought it would have mounted. *The True Tragedie.*	But when the imperial lion's flesh is gored, He rends and tears it with his wrathful paw, And highly scorning, that the lowly earth Should drink his blood, mounts up to the air. Marlow's *Edward II.*
Stern Falconbridge commands the narrow seas.—*Ibid.*	The haughty Dane commands the narrow seas.—*Ibid.*

I am, however, far from sure that the argument founded on these and other similarities between the *Contention* and the works of Marlow and of Greene, would not go to prove that some of the very additions to the old plays, in the *Second and Third Parts of King Henry VI*, with which Shakespeare is credited, were the work of one or other of his contemporaries. I give one example to show what I mean. In *The Second Part of Henry VI*, i. 3, occurs the line:

> She bears a duke's revenues on her back.

In the 4to, 1619, of *The First Part of the Contention*, the line stands thus:

> She bears a duke's whole revenues on her back;

but it is wholly wanting in the earlier editions; and it is this edition of 1619, which Mr. Halliwell regards as an intermediate version, presenting Shakespeare's first draft of *The Second Part of Henry VI.* Now this very addition is almost wholly the property of Marlow, for in his *Edward II,* we read—

> He wears a lord's revenue on his back.

Here then is an intricate problem. Was Marlow the amender of the old play of *The First Part of the Contention*? and was Shakespeare a purloiner from Marlow? Perhaps neither.

In order to show in what manner Shakespeare availed himself of the old plays of *The First Part of the Contention,* and *The True Tragedie,* I will adduce five passages from these plays, and place in juxtaposition with them the corresponding passages in *The Second and Third Parts of King Henry VI.* Further, with a view to afford the reader the means of appreciating the true character of the quarto edition of 1619, which contains both parts of the *Contention,* I have added the corresponding passages in this edition, which Mr. Halliwell regards as 'an intermediate composition.' I need only add that, with the exception of a passage containing the genealogy of the Duke of York, there is none other which countenances, or at least supports, Mr. Halliwell's view. The other variations are (as it seems to me) of no greater significance than the general run of various readings in the early quarto editions of Shakespeare, and which assuredly have no source more respectable than the blunders of printers and copyists, and the tinkerings of players.

(1.) *Humphrey.* This night when I was laid in bed, I dreampt that
This my staffe mine Office badge in Court,
Was broke in two, and on the ends were plac'd,
The heads of the Cardinall of *Winchester*,
And *William de la Poule* first Duke of Suffolke.

The First Part of the Contention, 4to, 1594.

This night when I was laid in bed, I dreamt
That this my staffe, mine office badge in Court,
Was broke in twaine, by whom I cannot gesse :
But as I thinke by the Cardinall.   What it bodes
God knowes ; and on the ends were plac'd
The heads of Edmund Duke of Somerset,
And William de la Pole first Duke of Suffolke.

Ibid., 4to, 1619.

Methought this staff, mine office-badge in Court,
Was broke in twain ; by whom I have forgot,
But as I think, it was by the Cardinal ;
And on the pieces of the broken wand
Were placed the heads of Edmund Duke of Somerset,
And William de la Pole, first Duke of Suffolk.
This was my dream : what it doth bode, God knows.

II Henry VI, folio, 1623.

(2.) *Elnor.* Ile come after you, for I cannot go before,
But ere it be long, Ile go before them all,
Despight of all that seeke to crosse me thus,

The First Part of the Contention, 4to, 1594.

Ile come after you, for I cannot go before,
As long as Gloster beares this base and humble minde :
Were I a man, and Protector as he is,
I'de reach to th' crowne, or make some hop headlesse.
And being but a woman, ile not behinde
For playing of my part, in spite of all that seek to crosse me thus :

Ibid., 4to, 1619.

> Yes, my good lord, I'll follow presently,
> Follow I must; I cannot go before,
> While Gloucester bears this base and humble mind.
> Were I a man, a duke, and next of blood,
> I would remove these tedious stumbling-blocks
> And smooth my way upon their headless necks;
> And being a woman, I will not be slack
> To play my part in Fortune's pageant.
> *II Henry VI*, folio, 1623.

(3.) And his proud wife, high minded *Elanor*,
That ruffles it with such a troupe of Ladies,
As strangers in the Court takes her for the Queene.
The First Part of the Contention, 4to, 1594.

> And his proud wife, high minded Elanor,
> That ruffles it with such a troupe of Ladies,
> As strangers in Court take her for the Queene;
> She beares a Dukes whole revennewes on her backe.
> *Ibid.*, 4to, 1619.

> Not all these lords do vex me half so much
> As that proud dame, the lord protector's wife.
> She sweeps it through the court with troops of ladies,
> More like an empress than Duke Humphrey's wife:
> Strangers in the court do take her for the queen:
> She bears a duke's revennues upon her back, etc.
> *II Henry VI*, folio, 1623.

(4.) I have seduste a headstrong Kentishman,
John Cade of Ashford,
Under the title of Sir John Mortemer,
To raise commotion, etc.
The First Part of the Contention, 4to, 1594.

> I have seduste a headstrong Kentish man,
> John Cade of Ashford,
> Under the title of Sir John Mortimer,
> (For he is like him every kinde of way)
> To raise commotion, etc. *Ibid.*, 4to, 1619.

> I have seduced a headstrong Kentish man,
> John Cade of Ashford,
> To make commotion, as full well he can,
> Under the title of John Mortimer.
>
> *II Henry VI*, folio, 1623.

(5.) *Clarence* beware, thou keptst me from the light,
But I will sort a pitchie daie for thee.
For I will buz abroad such prophesies,
As *Edward* shall be fearefull of his life,
And then to purge his feare, Ile be thy death.
Henry and his sonne are gone, thou Clarence next,
And one by one I will dispatch the rest,
Counting my selfe but bad, till I be best.
Ile drag thy bodie in another roome,
And triumph *Henry* in thy daie of doome.

The True Tragedie, 1595.

Clarence beware, thou keptst me from the light,
But I will sort a pitchie daie for thee.
For I will buz abroad such prophesies,
Under pretence of outward seeming ill,
As *Edward* shall be fearefull of his life,
And then to purge his feare, Ile be thy death.
King *Henry*, and the Prince his sonne are gone,
And *Clarence* thou art next to follow them,
So by one and one dispatching all the rest,
Counting my selfe but bad, till I be best.
Ile drag thy bodie in another roome,
And triumph *Henry* in thy daie of doom.

Ibid., 1619.

Clarence, beware; thou keep'st me from the light:
But I will sort a pitchy day for thee;
For I will buz abroad such prophecies
That Edward shall be fearfull of his life,
And then, to purge his feare, I'll be his death.

> King Henry and the prince his son are gone:
> Clarence thy turn is next, and then the rest,
> Counting myself but bad till I be best.
> I'll throw thy body in another room
> And triumph, Henry, in thy day of doom.
>
> *III Henry VI*, folio, 1623.

If Shakespeare had no hand in these two old plays, it is demonstrable that more than four-sevenths of those plays were borrowed, and appropriated *verbatim*, by Shakespeare, in the composition of the *Second and Third Parts of King Henry VI*. Mr. Halliwell, however, thinks it not unlikely that they are both *rifacimenti* by Shakespeare of older plays (*The First Sketches of II and III Henry VI*, edited by Halliwell for the Shakespeare Society, 1843, introd., p. 19), a conjecture which is unhappily unsupported by evidence, or it would relieve Shakespeare from the charge of appropriation. But we need not, I think, be very nice on that score, when we consider the large levies he made on contemporary *prose* literature.* I ought to add that we know of no old play corresponding to *The First Part of King Henry VI*. This default, considered in conjunction with the poverty of that performance, might incline one to think that it owes as little to the genius of

---

* Compare, for example, Shakespeare's Roman plays with North's *Plutarch:* take *Coriolanus* as a sample: or, better still, perhaps, consult Florio's *Montaigne*, and see how Shakespeare could appropriate a long and curious passage. In all such cases he made no attempt to stamp his own originality on what he borrowed; he simply touched it up, so as to make it serviceable to his needs, and fall into fair blank verse. In this art he certainly did not surpass Byron or Coleridge.

Shakespeare as do *The First Part of the Contention* and *The True Tragedie*.*

These four (or five) plays form a class by themselves. Into another class fall four other plays, which are almost universally received and always cited as first sketches by Shakespeare: these are as follows: *An excellent conceited Tragedie of Romeo and Juliet*, 4to, 1597; *The Chronicle Historie of Henry the Fifth*, 4to, 1600, 1602, and 1608; *A most pleasaunt and excellent conceited Comedie of Syr John Falstaffe, and the Merry Wives of Windsor*, 4to, 1602, and 1619; and *The Tragicall Historie of Hamlet, Prince of Denmark*, 4to, 1603.

These respectively correspond to *Romeo and Juliet, The Life of King Henry V, The Merry Wives of Windsor,* and *Hamlet*, of the folio collections. But though I have, for convenience, assigned these four sketches to one class, no two of them can be said to possess common characteristics. In the first place, I find it hard to believe that Shakespeare had the lion's share in the composition of the old *Romeo and Juliet*, and the old *Hamlet* bears abundant internal evidence of having been printed from a manuscript copy which had been fabricated out of the odds and ends furnished by an unskilled reporter. This play was entered on the books of the Stationers' Company in 1602, and so may have been acted some years before. It seems, however, not improbable that it was a *rifacimento* of

---

* Readers may consult with advantage the Harness Prize Essay for 1874, by Mr. G. L. Rives, which deals exclusively with the authorship of the three parts of *Henry VI*. His statements, however, contain some inaccuracies which endanger the soundness of his conclusions.

an older play; that it was the older *Hamlet* which was played at Henslow's theatre on June 9th, 1594, and that this was the play alluded to by Nash in his 'Epistle to the Gentlemen Students of the two Universities,' prefixed to Robert Greene's *Menaphon*, 1589, and also by Lodge in that eccentric brochure, entitled *Wit's Miserie, or the World's Madnesse*, 1596.* But these are questions which it is impossible to discuss in the compass of this paper.†

Into another class I must place the remaining four plays of those above cited, on which I will bestow but a passing remark. It is almost certain that John Fletcher wrote the greater part of *The Life of King Henry VIII.* The author of *Titus Andronicus* it is now impossible to determine. As far as I know it has never been satisfactorily made out that Shakespeare wrote any part of it. It must be admitted that all the external evidences give him the sole authorship, as indeed they do in the case of several plays universally allowed to be

* Oxberry, the player, in his acting edition of *Marlow's Dramatic Works*, 1818, asserts that in *Richard II*, Shakespeare has borrowed largely, 'and, to speak with candour, rather too largely,' from Marlow's *Edward II*. In support of this he cites from *Edward II* the scene in which Edward is required by Leicester and others to give up his crown; and 'the looking-glass scene' from *Richard II*, viz., that in which Richard is required by Bolingbroke and Northumberland to do the like. The passages are too long for quotation here, and, in my opinion, do not support Oxberry's charge. Nevertheless, Mr. A. C. Swinburne may be right in his view that Marlow's *Edward II* 'must undoubtedly be regarded as the immediate model of Shakespeare's *Richard II*.' (*Fortnightly Review*, May, 1875, p. 629).

† I cannot but believe that the allusion to *Hamlet* in *Sir Thomas Smithes Voiage and Entertainment in Rushia*, 1605; in Dekker's *Belman's Night Walks*, 1612; and in Rowlands' *Night Raven*, 1620, are also to the pre-Shakespearian drama.

spurious; but in this (as in those) the internal evidences wholly negative his claim. *Timon of Athens* is a joint composition, of which it is quite easy to determine the parts which were written by Shakespeare, and those which were written by another dramatist. As an example of this, take the two following speeches of Apemantus:

>   Hoyday,
> What a sweepe of vanitie comes this way.
> They daunce! They are madwomen,
> Like madnesse is the glory of this life,
> As this pompe shewes to a little oyle and roote.
> We make our selves fooles, to disport our selves,
> And spend our flatteries, to drinke those men,
> Upon whose age we voyde it up agen
> With poysonous spight and envy.
> Who lives, that's not depraved, or depraves?
> Who dyes, that beares not one spurne to their graves
> Of their friends guift?
> I should feare, those that daunce before me now,
> Would one day stampe upon me: 't has bene done,
> Men shut their doores against a setting sunne.

We may be quite sure that this is the older work. It has not the ring of Shakespeare in any of his moods: nay more, it has not a single feature, turn, or style which suggests him, and might, for aught I see to the contrary, have been written by one who bombasted it when Kyd and Marlow were in their swaddling clothes.* When Shakespeare condescends to

---

* Mr. Fleay is confident that this (Knight's) view is untenable. He writes, 'The un-Shaksperian parts were certainly the latest written.' Tr. N.S.S., 1874, P. I, p. 139. I am unconvinced. Some speeches in the play seem to me to be not only inferior but older work.

repair the old rubbish, see what sterling work he makes of it. Here is Shakespeare's Apemantus:

> what, think'st
> That the bleake ayre, thy boysterous chamberlaine,
> Will put thy shirt on warme? Will these moss'd trees,*
> That have out-liv'd the eagle, page thy heeles
> And skip when thou point'st out? Will the cold brooke
> Candied with ice, caudle thy morning taste
> To cure thy o're-nights surfet? Call the creatures,
> Whose naked natures live in all the spight
> Of wrekefull Heaven, whose bare unhoused trunkes,
> To the conflicting elements expos'd,
> Answer meere nature: bid them flatter thee.
> O thou shalt finde —— thou flatter'st misery.

Do you not here catch the rare old tones of him who sang the outcast king in the storm, and the banished duke in the forest of Ardenne? † The study of *Pericles* leads us to a similar conclusion, but the dissection is not so easy.‡

To these remarks I should add, that in *The Life and Death of King Richard II*, Shakespeare may have utilized an older play. Anyhow, there was at least *one* old play on this subject. Such a play was acted in 1601, and again in 1611.

In using up old materials, and graffing one play upon

---

* 'Moss'd trees' is Hanmer's reading. The folios have *moist trees*.

† After making this selection, I observed that Mr. Knight, in his *Studies of Shakespeare*, 1851, p. 72, had selected the same speeches for comparison; to which he adds two speeches of Flavius, the just steward, viz., that beginning, 'What will this come to?' and that beginning, 'If you suspect my husbandry.' These exhibit the double authorship almost as well as the former pair; but, of course, the grander is the character, the more striking is the contrast.

‡ Mr. Fleay takes the opposite view.

another, Shakespeare was merely conforming to an established usage. We can hardly regret that he did so, even though the practice is to be reprehended, as likely to give currency to falsehood. Be that as it may, we cannot but marvel at that magic skill, which at the first touch endows the grub with wings, and then transmutes it into a lovely butterfly. The material he used up seems mostly to have been the livelier portions of the old play-house stock, which, like the bones in a dust-heap, become the property of the first person who takes the trouble to turn them to account. Verily the poet must have wrought *ut magus*, who made those dry bones live.*

Justifiable or not, the practice was eminently advantageous; it not only effected a great economy in the playwright's mental resources and 'midnight oil,' but ensured for the audience the maintenance of their old interest in the story represented. I have elsewhere pointed out and established the low social status of the dramatist at this time.† Play-writing and acting were neither trades nor professions. When the Professor in *The Water Babies* caught Tom in his net, he called him an eft, but observing that he had no tail (so that he could not be an eft) and was to all appearance a land-baby (and therefore could not live under water), he let him go, and struck him out of the book of life. Like Tom, the Elizabethan players and

---

* *Ut magus;* two words from Horace (Ep. i., lib. ii. l. 213) which surmount the noble portrait of Shakespeare, attributed to Cornelius Jansen, the property of the Duke of Somerset.

† See *Was Thomas Lodge a player? An exposition touching the social status of the Dramatist in the reign of Elizabeth*, imp. 8vo, 1868; and *Shakspere Allusion-Books,* Part I, 'General Introduction,' p. iii.

dramatists 'fell between two stools.' Their patrons regarded them as persons *sans aveu*, and therefore statutable vagrants. Accordingly, it came to pass that where all was disreputable, no particular scandal arose from one dramatist *annexing* the lucubration or inspiration of another, unless, indeed, the preserve of one theatre were poached upon by the playwright of another. In that event fired out the smouldering jealousy which maintained the standing quarrels of rival theatres. To this wretched jealousy we are indebted for a most curious piece of evidence, that Shakespeare did some poaching at the Globe, whatever he may have done at Charlecote or Fulbrooke. I refer to the famous passage in *Greens Groatsworth of Wit bought with a Million of Repentance*, 1592, to which I shall shortly revert. *A propos* of that, Mr. Halliwell quotes from a quarto tract, dated 1594, called *Greene's Funeralls*, by R. B., Gent., 1594, the last couplet of the following stanza:

> Greene is the pleasing object of an eye,
> Greene pleased the eyes of all that looked upon him,
> Greene is the ground of every painter's dye,
> Greene gave the ground to all that wrote upon him.
> Nay more, the men that so eclipst his fame
> Purloin'd his plumes, can they deny the same?*

Shakespeare was certainly one of the men censured here.

* I have never seen a copy of this scarce book. For the complete stanza I am indebted to Mr. Rives' Harness-Prize Essay. The fourth line is misquoted by Mr. S. Neil in his *Biography of Shakespeare*, 4to, 1869, p. 22; and by myself in the *Shakspere Allusion-Books*, Part I, 1874, 'General Introduction,' p. xi. I copied from Mr. Neil. From whom did he copy?

I have called the more ancient Elizabethan plays, waifs from the general wreck of the older drama. In the coming days of Macaulay's New Zealander, the grander works of Shakespeare will remain to our posterity, not like waifs that have drifted down by reason of their lightness, but like the boulders which, by reason of their solidity and weight, have escaped the general denudation. Perhaps, too, in time to come, the Apollyon power of criticism may reveal Shakespeare's method of composition, by some subtle process of disintegration of which we now know nothing. I have marked, on the sea beach at Filey, the work of destruction which the tide is ceaselessly waging among the Oolitic rocks. The primeval sand had been amassed by the ancient sea in the usual rippled form, and thus became stratified. The sea is now silting out the less solid particles from the rock, and breaking it up into slabs, whose cleavage shows the old ripple-mark. 'Nature,' says Emerson, 'can never keep a secret;' she never wholly erases her footprints, and we may be sure that the genius of Shakespeare was not more subtle or cunning than nature.

Putting aside the questions suggested by the plays, it is necessary, for the completion of our inquiry, to ascertain what contemporary testimony is extant, which by identifying William Shakespeare, the player, with the author of the plays, may prevent or rebut all rational doubt on the subject. Any difficulty which we may meet with here more or less infects all the poetic literature of that day. For instance, the beautiful epigram on 'Sidney's sister, Pembroke's mother,' which is No. 15 in Ben Jonson's *Underwoods*, is also in a collection of poems by Jonson's friend, William Browne (*Lansdowne Manuscripts*, 777, first printed by Sir Egerton Brydges), with an additional verse. I suspect the second verse is all that belongs to Browne. The pastoral, 'Come live with me and be my love,' is assigned to Marlow in *England's Helicon*, 1600, and the nymph's reply, 'If love and all the world were young,' is there given to Raleigh, under the pseudonym IGNOTO: yet the first of these, and the first verse of the second, constitute No. 20 in the collection of short pieces attributed to Shakespeare, printed in 1599, and senselessly called *The Passionate Pilgrim*. No. 11 in the same collection, 'Venus with young Adonis sitting by her,' occurs in a volume called *Fidessa, a collection of Sonnets*, by B. Griffin, 1596, and Nos. 8. and 21, 'If Music and sweet Poetry agree,' and 'As it fell upon a day,' are included in a collection called *Poems in Divers Humors*, 1598, attributed to Richard Barnefeild. Who has sufficient knowledge to solve *these* questions of authorship? and *those* which relate to the drama are (for various reasons inapplicable to minor poetry) infinitely more intricate and perplexing.

There is a growing school which affects to disbelieve in Shakespeare's authorship of the works attributed to him. There were probably sceptics of this sort before 1852; but the earliest attempt to impugn the prevalent belief, so far as I know, was made in the number of *Chambers' Edinburgh Journal* for August 7th in that year. The spirit of the article is healthy enough. The scantiness of our evidence is fairly pointed out; at the same time, the two dedications to Lord Southampton, and the testimony of Jonson, both prose and verse, are admitted to weigh heavily against the doubters. On the other hand, the omission of all mention of Shakespeare from the works of Raleigh and Bacon is noticed, without the suggestion of their possible authorship of the works attributed to Shakespeare. The game thus started was hunted, by Miss Delia Bacon, in *Putnam's Monthly* for January, 1856 (vol. vii, p. 1). It is here that the claims of Lord Bacon to the authorship of those works were first advanced. In 1856, an original inquirer, Mr. William Henry Smith (then of Brompton, now or late of Highgate), published a letter to the first Lord Ellesmere, with the interrogative title, *Was Lord Bacon the Author of Shakespeare's plays?* This he followed up, in 1857, with a small volume on the same subject, entitled *Bacon and Shakespeare*. In the same year was published the enormous volume (the composition of which cost Miss Delia Bacon her reason and her life) called *The Philosophy of the Plays of Shakespeare unfolded*. In this book the joint claims of Raleigh and Bacon are advocated with the faith and earnestness of a martyr. Lastly, in 1866 was published in America a large volume entitled, *The Authorship of the Plays attributed to Shakespeare*, by Nathaniel Holmes, one of the Judges of the Supreme Court of the State of Missouri. This work is entirely devoted to the advocacy of Lord Bacon's authorship. Mr. Holmes having presented Mr. James Spedding, the editor of Bacon's works, with a copy of this book, and solicited his opinion thereupon, was so fortunate as to elicit an admirable criticism on the general question. This, together with other private letters which have passed between Messrs. W. H.

Smith, Spedding, and Holmes, I have been permitted to read, but I am not at liberty to make known their very curious contents.*

This remarkable controversy is not without its uses. It serves to call particular attention to the existence of a class of minds which, like Macadam's sieves, retain only those ingredients that are unsuited to the end in view. Mix up a quantity of matters relevant and irrelevant, and those minds will eliminate from the instrument of reasoning every point on which the reasoning ought to turn, and then proceed to exercise their constitutional perversity on the residue. This is the class of minds to which Bishop Warburton belonged; so that what Thomas De Quincey (*Works*, A. & C. Black, vol. vi, p. 259) writes of that prelate will serve for a generic description:

> The natural vegetation of his intellect tended to that kind of fungus which is called 'crochet;' so much so that if he had a just and powerful thought (as sometimes in germ he had), or a wise and beautiful thought, yet by the mere perversity of his tortuous brain, it was soon digested into a crochet.

The profession of the law (which at first was Warburton's) has (as De Quincey perceived) the inevitable effect of fostering the native tendency of such minds. For a fresh field of

---

* This correspondence has been since published as an appendix to the third edition of Judge Holmes' work, issued in 1876. Other works on this curious controversy are—*William Shakspere not an Impostor*, 1857; *Who wrote Shakspere?* by J. V. P. (*Fraser's Magazine*, August, 1874); *Bacon versus Shakespeare, a Plea for the Defendant*, by J. D. King, 1875; and *The Shakespeare-Bacon Controversy*, by E. O. Vaile, 1875 (*Scribner's Monthly*, April, 1875).

studying their idiosyncrasy we are indebted to this controversy. It has also another use. It incites us to look up our evidences for Shakespeare's authorship; and we are reminded how few and meagre they are.

The critic has the same interest in the works of Miss Delia Bacon, Mr. W. H. Smith, and Judge Holmes, as the physician has in morbid anatomy. He reads them, not so much for the light which they throw on the question of authorship, as for their interest as examples of wrong-headedness. It is not at all a matter of moment whether Bacon, Raleigh, or another be the favourite on whom the works are fathered; but it is instructive to discover by what plausible process the positive evidences of Shakespeare's authorship (scanty as they are) are put out of court. As to Bacon as first favourite, I suppose anyone conversant with the life and authentic works of that powerful but unamiable character, must agree with Mr. Spedding's judgment, that, unless he be the author of "Shakespeare," neither his life nor his writings give us any assurance that he could excel as a dramatic poet. Of all men who have left their impress on the reign of the first maiden Queen, not one can be found who was so deficient in human sympathies as Lord Bacon. As for such a man portraying a woman in all her natural simplicity, purity, and grace; as to his imagining and bodying forth in natural speech and action such exquisite creations as Miranda, Perdita, Cordelia, Desdemona, Marina—the supposition is the height of absurdity. What, as it seems to me, has led astray the few writers who have set up a claim for Lord Bacon, is his admirable gift of language, scarcely inferior to that of Shakespeare himself.* This almost unique endowment caused Bacon to manifest a kind of likeness to Shakespeare in matters into which the sympathies of the man and the training of the dramatic poet do not enter. Hence it is easy to cull from the works of these two great masters a considerable number of curious parallels. I have looked over the collections of Messrs. W. H. Smith and Holmes, and I must confess I am astonished; but my astonishment has not been provoked by the quantity or closeness of the resemblances adduced, but by the spectacle of educated men attempting to found such an edifice on such a foundation. I could from my own reading add to their collections some remarkable parallelisms which they have overlooked.† But what of that? Is there anything singular in the case? Not at all. For if parallelisms can prove identity of authorship, what an array of anonymous plays ought to be put to Shakespeare's credit! For instance, the old play of *Lust's Dominion* has no owner: in the course of its perusal, I observed some very remarkable parallels between its text and that of

---

* Unquestionably Mr. Tennyson is the most richly endowed, in this respect, of all the poets of our day; a fact which was adroitly turned to his disadvantage by the late Lord Lytton, who sneeringly said, 'Tennyson is a poet with a great vocabulary.'

† For instance, compare the following:

'And because the breath of flowers is far sweeter in the air (where it comes and goes, like the warbling of music) than in the hand,' etc.—*Essay* lxvi.

      O, it came o'er my ear, like the sweet sound
      That breathes upon a bank of violets;
      Stealing and giving odour.—*Twelfth Night*, i, 1.

Shakespeare. I will mention two by way of illustration. In act i, scene 1, the Moor, speaking of the multitude, asks the Queen-mother,

> Who arms this many-headed beast, but you?

Compare this with *Coriolanus*, act iv, scene 1—

> The beast
> With many heads butts me away.

and with the Induction to *II Henry IV*,

> ——the blunt monster with uncounted heads,
> The still-discordant waving multitude.

Again, the Queen-mother, at the end of the play (act v, scene 3), when all her troubles are consummated, says,

> I'll now repose myself in peaceful rest,
> And fly into some solitary residence,
> Where I'll spin out the remnant of my life,
> In true contrition for my past offences:

a passage which reminds us of Paulina's last speech in *A Winter's Tale*, somewhat as a flowered tea-tray reminds us of a garden.

How many of such resemblances think you between *Lust's Dominion* and Shakespeare would prove the right of that play to a place in the received collection? My answer is that a large number of such cases would assuredly dispose of that claim, and a small number would go no way to prove it. It requires no minute acquaintance with Shakespeare's text for a reader to be struck with that inexhaustible pregnancy of language which rarely repeats an image once expressed, without expressing it anew. In fact it is one argument against Shakespeare's authorship of *The Two Noble Kinsmen*, which has his name, along with Fletcher's, on the title, that so many Shakespearianisms occur in its text.

> And I . . . .
> Doe here present this Machine, or this frame.
> *Two Noble Kinsmen*, iii, 6.
>
> Thou mighty one, that with thy power has turn'd
> Green Neptune into purple.
> *Ibid.*, v, 1.
>
> PALAMON (*addressing* MARS).
> Thou great decider
> Of dusty and old titles, that heal'st with blood
> The earth when it is sick, and cur'st the world
> O' the *pluresie* of people.
> *Ibid.*, v, 1.

And yet we are asked to believe that, because Bacon writes, 'All was *inned* at last unto the King's barn,' and 'the cold becometh more *eager*,' therefore he was the author of *All's Well that Ends Well* and *Hamlet*.

Summarily disallowing, then, the claims set up on behalf of Bacon, I proceed to consider, with the utmost brevity, those evidences on which we are justified in attributing to Shakespeare the chief authorship of the dramas which have the passport of his name. I own at the outset that those evidences are scanty: not so scanty as Mr. W. H. Smith would have us believe, for he cites but four witnesses whose testimony was given in or close upon Shakespeare's lifetime, viz., Francis Meres (1598); William Basse (1622 *circa*); the anonymous author of *The Return from Pernassus* (1606, said to have been acted in 1602), and Ben Jonson. In fact, there are at least eleven besides; two of whom are among our chief witnesses.*

But so little weight do I attach to contemporary rumour as an evidence of authorship, that I shall trouble you with seven witnesses only. Of these, there are but four who directly identify the man, or the actor, with the writer of the plays and poems.

The first witness I shall call is John Harrison, the publisher; though it is but little that he can tell us. It was for him that *Venus and Adonis* was printed in 1593, and *Lucrece* in 1594. No author's name is on the title-page of either. But fortunately he prefixed to each a dedication to Lord Southampton, subscribed 'William Shakespeare.' It is to me quite incredible that Harrison would have done this, unless Shakespeare had

---

* I do not count Spenser, for the oft-quoted line from his *Tears of the Muses*,
'Our pleasant Willy, ah! is dead of late,'
unquestionably referred to Sir Philip Sydney, who (like some other poets) was alluded to under the pastoral name of Willy. Thus, in an eclogue signed A. W., in the *Poetical Rhapsody* quoted by Mr. Collier, in his Introduction to *Seven English Poetical Miscellanies*, 1867, occurs the following, in reference to Sydney's recent death:

We deem'd our Willy aye should live,
So sweet a sound his pipe could give;
  But cruell death
  Hath stopt his breath:
Dumb lies his pipe that wont so sweet to sound!

Besides, as Mr. Halliwell argues, Spenser's allusion could not be to Shakespeare; for the *Tears of the Muses* was probably written about 1580, though it was not published till ten years later. Shakespeare was but sixteen years old in 1580, and was not known in London *as a poet* till eight or nine years afterwards.

written the dedications, or at least had been a party to them. Now in dedicating the first poem, the undersigned speaks of it as 'my unpolisht lines,' and 'the first heir of my invention,' and he promises to honour his patron 'with some graver labour:' in dedicating the second poem he speaks of it as 'my untutored lines,' and adds, 'what I have done is yours, what I have to do is yours, being part in all I have, devoted yours.'

So far, then, we have a tittle of evidence to prove that one William Shakespeare was the author of both these poems. Three or four years later a well-known man of letters, named Francis Meres, speaks of Shakespeare as the author of *Venus and Adonis*, *Lucrece*, sundry sonnets, and ten specified plays. Of these plays nine are known to us and received as Shakespeare's. Meres' testimony is given in seven pages of his book, called *Palladis Tamia, Wit's Commonwealth*, 1598; but I have never seen quoted any of his remarks on Shakespeare's works, except the stock passages on folios 281 and 282, which one writer evidently borrows from another, to save himself the trouble of consulting the original. It is especially noteworthy that on the first page of folio 280, Meres selects Sir Philip Sidney, Spenser, Daniel, Drayton, Warner, Shakespeare, Marlow and Chapman, as the poets by whom the English tongue was 'mightily enriched, and gorgeouslie invested in rare ornaments and resplendent abiliments;' and it is evident from subsequent remarks that he awarded the palm to the authors of the *Faerie Queen* and the *Countess of Pembroke's Arcadia*.

Robert Greene (the abler and better known of the two Elizabethan poets of that surname) wrote a number of plays in conjunction with Marlow, Lodge, Nash and others, which had great popularity before the advent of Shakespeare. In his last publication, called *A Groatsworth of Wit Bought with a Million of Repentance,* 1592, he addresses an admonition to three of his associates, exhorting them to abandon playwriting. These we may readily identify as Marlow, Nash and Peele. Then follow the words, so often quoted, which are for us the important testimony:

> Base minded men al three of you, if by my miserie ye be not warned: for unto none of you (like me) sought those burres to cleave: those Puppits (I meane) that speake from our mouths, those Anticks garnisht in our colours. . . . Yes, trust them not: for there is an upstart Crow, beautified with our feathers, that with his *Tygers heart wrapt in a Players hide,* supposes he is as well able to bumbast out a blanke verse as the best of you:—

so far it might be conjectured that Shakespeare is the man alluded to: providentially Greene adds these words, which almost convert that conjecture into a certainty:

> and being an absolute *Johannes fac totum,* is in his owne conceit the onely Shake-scene in a countrie.

Burs, puppets, antics, crows in [peacock's] feathers—such are the hard words he gives the players; and these he follows up with a second instalment of abusive epithets—*apes, rude grooms, buckram gentlemen, peasants, and painted monsters!* *

---

* These were but conventional terms: so John Davies of Hereford has *apish actors, men more base,* &c.; Thomas Heywood, *puppets, painted images,* &c.; Robert Burton, *butterflies, baboons, apes,* and *antics;* and so forth.

Now in turning this extract to account, we must be more cautious than dramatic critics usually are to avoid reasoning in a circle. If we are fully satisfied that 'Shake-scene' contains a pun upon Shakespeare (and that independently of the verse), we may infer, perhaps, that Greene, or one of the dramatists admonished by him, wrote the whole or a part of *The True Tragedy of Richard, Duke of York*, and that Shakespeare pillaged his predecessor's work to 'beautifie,' or rather to fabricate, his Third Part of *Henry VI*. Anyhow, the line travestied occurs in both *The True Tragedy* and *The Third Part of Henry VI*.

The conclusion being reached that Shakespeare is the player assailed by Greene, the testimony of Henry Chettle, the editor of *Greene's Groatsworth of Wit*, is invested with a curious and special interest. Immediately after the appearance of that book, Chettle published a work of fiction called *Kind-Hart's Dreame*. In the preface to this he refers to the preceding work, and confesses to having expunged from the manuscript some of Greene's hard words: but he protests that he added nothing to it. After remarking on the admonition to the three dramatists he adds this splutter of solecisms:

> The other, whome at that time I did not so much spare, as since I wish I had, for that as I have moderated the heate of living writers, and might have usde my owne discretion (especially in such a case), the Author beeing dead, that I did not, I am as sory as if the originall fault had beene my fault, because my selfe have seene his demeanor no lesse civill, than he exelent in the qualitie he professes: Besides, divers of worship have reported his uprightnes of dealing, which argues his honesty, and his facetious grace in writting, that aprooves his Art.

This is indeed a singular apology. We may picture to our mind's eye the shadowless man, the tinker of old plays, the second-rate actor, who had already, like one of his heroes,

> bought
> Golden opinions from all sorts of people,

but who as yet had not become a man of worship, and an armiger in right of gentle blood, by the mere force of his unpretending frankness, modesty and gentleness, disarming his jealous and contemptuous traducers; insomuch that the respectable Henry Chettle, who had never been a motley and a vagrant, is prompted to give the author of *Hamlet* an acceptable testimonial. For my part, I honour Chettle for this tardy act of justice.

I suppose I must, in the next place, cite the ostensible editors of the first collection of Shakespeare's works; for they were none other than Heminge and Condell, two of the company who at the accession of James the First played under the joint management of Lawrence Fletcher and William Shakespeare. But, unfortunately for their credit and our satisfaction, their prefatory statement contains, or at least suggests, what they must have known to be false. They would lead us to believe that their edition was printed from Shakespeare's manuscripts:

> Who, as he was a happie imitator of Nature, was a most gentle expresser of it. His mind and hand went together: And what he thought, he uttered with that easinesse, that wee have scarse received from him a blot in his papers.

Now we have positive knowledge of a fact inconsistent with this excerpt. We know that the texts of eight of the plays in that edition were printed from the early quarto editions,* which they denounce as stolen and surreptitious, 'maimed, and deformed by the frauds and stealthes of injurious impostors,' and which plays they now offer 'cur'd and perfect of their limbes.' But notwithstanding this, the testimony of Shakespeare's fellows must be allowed to have some weight in the question of authorship. It is to me incredible that they should in that matter have attempted a fraud which must have been transparent to the noble brothers who lent their patronage to the volume, and which must sooner or later have been exposed in the face of all England.

Our last and principal witness is Ben Jonson, though he is less communicative than might have been expected considering the closeness of his friendship with Shakespeare. In what he writes of the man he seems to take it for granted that we know all about him already, and the things he tells us are not those we most want to know. There are the verses prefixed to the first folio of Shakespeare, and the remarks entitled, *De Shakespeare nostrati*, in his posthumous work called *Timber; or Discoveries made upon Men and Matter*. These remarks must be read in connection with Heminge and Condell's preface to the first folio, and with the Induction to Ben Jonson's play, entitled *The Staple of News*. In the latter,

* Viz., *Richard II, The First Part of King Henry IV, Love's Labour's Lost, Much Ado about Nothing, Romeo and Juliet, Titus Andronicus, A Midsummer Night's Dream,* and *The Merchant of Venice.*

Expectation says to Prologue, 'Sir, I can expect much.' Prologue answers, 'I fear too much, lady; and teach others to do the like.' Expectation rejoins, 'I can do that, too, if I have cause.' Upon which Prologue says, 'Cry you mercy, you never did wrong, but with just cause.' Truly one would never have found any evidence for Shakespeare in that, but for the explanation which Ben vouchsafes in his *Timber*. He writes :

> I remember, the Players have often mentioned it as an honour to *Shakespeare*, that in his writing, (whatsoever he penn'd) he never blotted out [? one] line. My answer hath beene, would he had blotted a thousand. Which they thought a malevolent speech. I had not told posterity this, but for their ignorance, who choose that circumstance to commend their friend by, wherein he most faulted : and to justifie mine owne candor, (for I lov'd the man, and doe honour his memory (on this side idolatry) as much as any). Hee was (indeed) honest, and of an open, and free nature : had an excellent *Phantsie*, brave notions, and gentle expressions : wherein hee flow'd with that facility, that sometime it was necessary he should be stop'd : *Sufflaminandus erat ;* as *Augustus* said of *Haterius*. His wit was in his owne power ; would the rule of it had beene so too. Many times hee fell into those things, could not escape laughter : As when he said in the person of *Cæsar*, one speaking to him ; *Cæsar thou dost me wrong.* Hee replyed : *Cæsar did never wrong, but with just cause:* and such like ; which were ridiculous. But hee redeemed his vices, with his virtues. There was ever more in him to be praysed then to be pardoned.

This is direct testimony, not merely to the fact that Shakespeare wrote the play of *Julius Cæsar*, but that Cæsar's reply to Metellus Cimber was—

> Cæsar did never wrong but with just cause,
> Nor without cause will he be satisfied.

But of course the editors will not have it. It is proverbial that office is a strong perverter of the judgment. It would seem as if a critic became blear-eyed so soon as he turned editor.

We may, I think, unreservedly accept the whole of Ben's testimony in *this* matter. Probably, the five couplets, which he wrote on Droeshout's engraved portrait of Shakespeare prefixed to the early folios, are merely complimentary, for they convey but a trite and common sentiment.* I do not, however, rely on them as an evidence of authorship, but on the forty couplets which follow the preface to the Folio 1623, addressed by Ben 'To the memory of my beloved, the Author, Mr. William Shakespeare : and what he hath left us.' These verses are a precious testimony, both to the authorship of the plays and to Ben's friendly estimate of the author's genius. But forasmuch as they do not deal in specialities I have no occasion to quote them at length. It is curious that one of the phrases of eulogy here employed is repeated by Ben almost *totidem verbis* in a note entitled ' Scriptorum Catalogus,' in his *Timber;* but it is there applied to Lord Bacon. To Shakespeare he says—

> O, when thy socks were on,
> Leave thee alone, for the comparison
> Of all, that insolent Greece, or haughtie Rome
> Sent forth, etc.

Of Bacon he writes—

* On this matter see *Shakespeare's Centurie of Prayse*, 1874, p. 169.

he who hath filled up all numbers, and performed that in our tongue which may be compared or preferred either to insolent Greece, or haughty Rome.

Of course the heretics have not been slow to avail themselves of this resemblance. They are welcome to what it is worth.

The conclusion which I think we may safely draw from the evidences adduced is, that no other known name is entitled to the credit awarded by common consent to 'William Shakespeare,' unless we go back to the playwrights who preceded him, and are able to identify the authors of those plays on which Shakespeare founded so many of his. In this case a residual problem is presented to us of so great difficulty, that at present no approximation has been made to its solution, and though it is one which has a special interest for me and comes within the scope of my subject its treatment would require the monopoly of a separate paper. *

Certain it is that in a considerable number of the plays (I think more than one-half) Shakespeare's all-assimilating genius derives its *pabulum* from the clumsy productions of earlier writers. To get an adequate notion of Shakespeare's art in this sort of work, I commend to your attention the play of *King John*, in comparison with *The Troublesome Reign*, and I shall be much surprised if you do not acquire an entirely new notion of Shakespeare's dramatic talent.

---

* Since this was written an 'approximation' has been arrived at in the case of, at least, six plays. The 'separate paper,' which was then a vague possibility, is now an actuality, and will be found in the second part of this work.

If I might venture to express my own opinion on this difficult inquiry, I should say, that in all probability, several of the comedies (strictly so called), and of the tragedies, *Macbeth*, *Coriolanus*, and *Julius Cæsar*, are not indebted to any older plays on the same subject;* and that *Antony and Cleopatra*, and the *Tempest*, are, in the profoundest sense, original compositions, the entire structure, as well as the architecture of each play, being wholly due to Shakespeare's incomparable art. Looking at those three plays only, unless, indeed, my judgment has been warped by force of habit, I there discern the figure of a poet who was of a more 'select and generous chief' than any of the imaginative writers of Elizabeth's reign. Hazlitt, who proclaimed Shakespeare's intellectual and æsthetic superiority to the men of that day, qualified his verdict by saying that 'it was a common and a noble brood.' With Mr. Alexander Dyce, let me say that 'falser remark was never made by critic.' That the times were curiously favourable to genius may be allowed; and we may agree with Goethe's opinion, that much of what the giants of those days became and achieved was due to the 'stimulating atmosphere' in which they lived.† None can say to what forest trees the garden flowers of our day, such as Tennyson and Browning, might have waxed, had they been planted in an

---

* Since this was written the Rev. F. G. Fleay has made an unfortunate attempt to fix on both *Macbeth* and *Julius Cæsar* the brand of double authorship. Nevertheless I think very highly of his labours in the cases of *Timon of Athens* and *Pericles*.

† I observe a similar remark in Emerson's Essay on *Eloquence*, in his *Letters and Social Aims*, 1876, p. 117.

Elizabethan soil. But if so much be due to a man's surroundings, we must also admit with sorrow, that the direction into which the energies of Englishmen have been diverted is not only unfavourable but fatal to artistic life, and that an artist of Shakespeare's stamp will never more be possible among us :—

'We ne'er shall look upon his like again.'

CHAPTER V.

THE PORTRAITURE OF SHAKESPEARE.*

THE title of my paper may well provoke this question—'Seeing that Shakespeare has been dead and buried 257 years, what can be known of his personal appearance beyond what may be gathered from the few accredited portraits, for which he is believed to have sat? and granting that all those are unsatisfactory and imperfect representations of the man, how is it possible to add to their verisimilitude, except by the discovery of another authentic portrait?' Of course I do not pretend that this *is* possible; nor am I able to announce to you any discovery of the sort since 1849, when the Becker Mask was deposited at the British Museum. Nevertheless I have somewhat to communicate, which may be both new and interesting, touching certain recent attempts to recover the lost lineaments of Shakespeare,

   And steal dead seeming of his living hue. †

---

 * Read at a Meeting of the Royal Society of Literature, Jan. 21, 1874, and reported (in brief) in the Presidential Address of 1874, p. 50.
 † From Shakespeare's sixty-seventh Sonnet.

Doubtless the chances are against the success of such attempts: but it is not difficult to see that in one respect at least they may be helpful and instructive. If we only consider what a bust or a portrait must be in order to express the 'form and favour' of a man at his best, we shall readily arrive at a principle, which, while it serves to explain that diversity of expression which is found in different copies from the same picture, to some extent justifies the attempt to recover a lost likeness.

I have frequently observed that the 'portrait of a gentleman,' painted by an indifferent artist, bears a certain resemblance to the artist himself. In the Epistle of St. James it is asserted that a man 'beholding his natural face in a glass, goeth his way and straightway forgetteth what manner of man he was.' I am not sure that this is strictly true; but, if it be so, I am none the less convinced that every man has a latent impression of his own countenance, which he is more apt to delineate than any other. Moreover, I have observed that in portraits, executed by the best artists and possessing all the attributes of a faithful likeness, there is always an expression which it is impossible to attribute to anything seen in the face of the sitter. The truth seems to be, that the artist who has studied his subject, so as to seize the expression of the face at its best, is dependent upon his own powers of imagination and memory: and on these he draws largely to supplement the expression of the blank and wearied face which periodically confronts him in his studio. It thus happens that in representing his subject he imparts something of himself, and the most life-like portraits are those which represent the very heart of the painter.

On this principle we can clearly understand how it comes to pass that of all the known engravings of Jansen's portrait of Shakespeare, in the collection of the Duke of Somerset, there are not two that have the same expression. But the Chandos portrait, which is the property of the nation, from its damaged condition and obscurity offers a still better field for experiment. It has been engraved and copied in oils times without number, and so different are the expressions of the resulting prints and paintings that it is difficult to believe that they are all from the same exemplar. I can certify as a fact that Cousins' engraving is a remarkably faithful copy of the original. Now compare it with Scriven's print of Ozias Humphry's drawing, and it is difficult to resist the conclusion that the fire and severity of this last are wholly due to the temperament of the copyist. It is well known that William Blake could conjure up before him the visible forms of the dead, and retain them long enough to paint their likenesses. From some of these we may conclude that the latent memory of ancient portraits was at least a factor in this singular phenomenon; but the portraits of 'the Man who built the Pyramids' and 'the Ghost of a Flea' do not so readily yield to this explanation. You will perhaps call to mind an incident related by the elder Varley respecting the portraiture of 'the Ghost of a Flea.' The old man was present during the 'sitting,' and he relates that, the Flea having opened his mouth, Blake was unable at once to complete the drawing, but drew on a separate piece of paper a sketch of the open mouth. The apparition having once more closed his mouth, Blake resumed the first sketch, and finished the portrait. This seems a veritable case of portrait-painting from the inmost consciousness: and what is most curious about Blake's portrait of 'the Ghost of a Flea' is that it is a caricature of the well-known features of the late Lord Lytton.

However ridiculous may appear the notion that Blake could summon into his presence the forms and faces of persons no longer existing, or those whose existence is impossible, and could draw from them, as from real flesh and blood, I am convinced from my own experience that Blake gave a truthful account of the matter, and that he was wholly unconscious of the process by which such appearances were produced. That process, which is a sort of concurrence of imagination with certain states of the brain and the optic nerve, probably affecting the retina in as perfect a manner as the light from natural objects, is unconsciously performed by all persons who have the experience of optical illusions.

Now that very constructive power, which in the case of Blake was at times monopolised by the nerves of vision, may just as well act through the hand, and, instead of presenting an illusory object which the artist may delineate or depict may guide him unconsciously in the production of an ideal portrait. Such things are called 'spirit drawings,' which I regard as a most misleading title. But without entering upon that allied, if not strictly relevant, inquiry, I may state generally that every genial portrait owes perhaps as much to the ideal of the artist as to his faculty of faithful representation; and that he works from within as well as from without. Herein lies the justification of the attempts that are made from time to time to produce a thoroughly satisfactory portrait of Shakespeare. In this pursuit we have little to guide us beyond a few portraits of somewhat doubtful authenticity and of very short pedigrees, the bust in the Chancel of Stratford Church and Droeshout's engraving prefixed to the First Folio Edition of Shakespeare. Beyond the suggestion of these generally inadequate and discrepant representations we have no guidance from without.

Unfortunately for our inquiry Shakespeare does not stand on the same footing as other great men of his time. He is *sui generis*, that is, of a class by himself in every respect. There is scarcely a poet above mediocrity who has not written commendatory verses on his fellows. We do not know of a single copy of such verses by Shakespeare. Allusions to his contemporaries are to be found in the writings of every other poet and dramatist of that day; some poems and plays are obtrusively crowded with such personal allusions. In the whole thirty-seven dramas credited to Shakespeare there is one obscure allusion to Spenser and one distinct allusion to Marlow. The prose works published in the later part of the sixteenth, and the earlier part of the seventeenth centuries contain abundant notices of every poet of mark save Shakespeare, whose name and works are rarely and only slightly mentioned: and when he is named or alluded to he is praised as an amatory poet or as an actor, rarely as a dramatist. The works of Lord Brooke,

Sir John Davies, Lord Bacon, Selden, Sir John Beaumont, Henry Vaughan (Silurist), Lord Clarendon, &c., &c., show no consciousness of Shakespeare's existence. Can it be that the poor player was evidently despised; that he was too humble to be selected as the subject of much eulogy in those early times, or to be invited to become the eulogist of another? For the same reason, whatever it was, hardly anyone cared to possess his portrait; and until John Aubrey records in 1680, *i. e.*, sixty-four years after Shakespeare's death, that he was reputed to have been 'a handsome, well-shaped man,' no writer ever said a word as to his personal appearance. It is but fair to add, that as to portraits, Edmund Spenser stands in precisely the same position as Shakespeare. The portraits claimed for him are hopelessly discrepant; and it is hard to say which should be accepted and which rejected. If we reckon up all the painted portraits (excluding known forgeries) said to represent Shakespeare, we shall find that their number is about twenty-two. Some of these, at most two or three, may have been taken from life; and certainly one is of the requisite antiquity. Not a few, however, are probably genuine portraits of other gentlemen of the time; and some are idealised portraits of Shakespeare. To these must be added two busts, one plaster cast and one engraving on brass; and we have reckoned up our whole capital. A very few words on some of these relics.

Foremost in authenticity is the Bust in the Chancel of Stratford Church. We know quite enough about this to make it our most important possession. Apart from what we know, it is *a priori* most improbable that the family and friends of Shakespeare should soon after his death have placed in the most conspicuous place in the church of his native town, where almost every one was as familiar with his personal appearance as with that of their most intimate friends, a life-sized bust of the Bard which would not be recognised by his fellow-townsmen. We might, in the absence of any relative knowledge, presume that the bust is a likeness. But we know from Sir William Dugdale that it was the work of a Dutch sculptor named Gerard Johnson; and we know enough of this sculptor to believe that he was not a common mason, though certainly quite a second-rate artist. We all know wherein such an one fails, and wherein he succeeds: he can usually make an obtrusively striking likeness, though always an unpleasant one. Here is just such a work. How awkward is the *ensemble* of the face! What a painful stare, with its goggle eyes and gaping mouth! The expression of this face has been credited with *humour, bonhommie, hilarity* and *jollity*. To me it is decidedly *clownish;* and is suggestive of a man crunching a sour apple, or struck with amazement at some unpleasant spectacle. Yet there is force in the lineaments of this muscular face. One can hardly doubt that it is an unintentional caricature; but for that very reason it should be an unmistakeable likeness. In the plaster casts taken from Bullock's copy, and in those separately prepared from the original by Warner and Michele, that peculiar expression is toned down to insipidity, and one catches some touch of dignity and refinement with utter loss of force. But the casts do not give a truthful representation of the bust.

We obtain some important facts from this rude work. As it is at present coloured the eyes are light-hazel, the hair and beard auburn. Such were the colours put on in 1748 by Mr. John Hall, the limner of Stratford, and which reappeared on the removal, by Mr. Collins, of Malone's white paint. We have no reason to doubt that when the bust was renovated in 1748, the very colours it had received by order of Dr. John Hall, Shakespeare's son-in-law, were repeated by his namesake.

The extraordinary depth of the upper lip, which measures an inch and a quarter, has been accounted for by the conjecture that the sculptor may have had an accident with the nose. I have remarked that it is very dangerous to frame hypotheses respecting Shakespeare, for they are apt to get converted into 'obscure traditions,' and may come at last to be regarded as historical facts, the evidence of which has been lost. This happened to the conjecture of Capell and Waldron that Shakespeare was lame, in order to explain two lines in the sonnets, the meaning of which he had wholly misapprehended. In the next century Mr. Harness revised the conjecture, without any mention of Capell; Mr. Thoms accounted for the supposed defect by making Shakespeare a soldier: and finally the late Mr. Richard Simpson published a note in which he referred the circumstance of Shakespeare's lameness to 'an obscure tradition,' and proceeded to employ it as a fact to elucidate some expressions in Jonson's *Poetaster*. Just so, in the matter of Shakespeare's nose; Mr. J. Hain Friswell remarks (*Life Portraits*, p. 8): 'the nose of the bust of Shakespeare, like that of Tristram Shandy, it is said, has met with an accident, the former from the instrument of Dr. Slop, the latter from the chisel of the sculptor.' 'It is said,' is the magical *formula*, which becomes the germ of the myth. I cannot find that it ever was said, except as a hypothesis to explain the disproportionate depth of the upper lip: and on measurement, it was found that the depth of Sir Walter Scott's upper lip exceeded that of Shakespeare's bust.

I am afraid we must take our stand on the fidelity of this bust—at least with some allowable qualifications. When we find a sculptor dismissing his work in this rough fashion, so that, as Mr. Fairholt says, 'the eyes are untrue to nature, &c., the ciliary cartilages are straight, hard and unmeaning, and the glands at the corners next the nose entirely omitted,' we may be sure the fidelity of the face must be received with something more than the proverbial grain of salt.

Next in authenticity to the bust is Droeshout's engraving, prefixed to the First Folio edition of Shakespeare's Works. It must have been executed after Shakespeare's death; and therefore we may be sure it was taken from some sketch or painting, probably in the possession of Mrs. Shakespeare or Dr. John Hall. No such exemplar has come down to us or is known to have existed, unless the Felton Portrait be the one that was so employed; and this is, on the whole, unlikely, for reasons to be stated when I come to speak of that portrait. But allowing the probability that such an exemplar did exist (and apart from it, no reliance could be placed on the engraving), it may have perished along with Shakespeare's papers. It has been surmised that these papers fell a victim to some pious soul's puritanical ardour. Unhappily the suspicion, if it be to fall anywhere, involves Shakespeare's wife or Shakespeare's daughter. The sorry Latin elegiacs engraved in brass on Mrs. Shakespeare's gravestone contain no allusion to her immortal husband, being concerned only with the good lady's immortality. She must not be held responsible for them; at least no further than she justified their encomium. The English verses on Mrs. Elizabeth Hall's tablet are enigmatical.

> Witty above her sexe, but that's not all,
> Wise to salvation was good Mistris Hall:
> Something of Shakespeare was in that, but this
> Wholy of him with whom she's now in blisse.

The things compared are Mrs. Hall's supersexual wit, and her wisdom to salvation. Which is 'that,' and which is 'this?' In strictness '*hic* plerumque ad posterius, *ille* ad prius refertur:' so that the lines seem to say, she owed her wit partly to Shakespeare; her piety wholly to him, with whom she is in bliss. Meanwhile where is her mother? It has been suggested that the lines mean the reverse, 'this' and 'that' being transposed for the sake of the rhyme: viz., that she owed her piety in some degree to Shakespeare; her wit wholly to him: but that would seem to make the wit her claim to salvation. Another suggestion is, that *him* refers to the Saviour; and I incline to that view myself: at the same time I am afraid we are inquiring too curiously in putting these old epitaphs to the question; and I do not think they tell at all against Mrs. Shakespeare. Probably both Mrs. Shakespeare and Mrs. Hall were good religious souls, but one does not see why either of them should be ashamed of the Bard, so as to disown his works and destroy his manuscripts. There is one curious fact, however, which is quite enough to beget a myth, like those of Shakespeare's lameness and his bust's broken nose. Heminge and Condell had the plays printed from the quartos and playhouse copies; they even had a title-page printed with the date 1622. They may have hoped to be able to correct the press from manuscripts left by Shakespeare at New Place, in the custody of his widow. Now the facts are, that Mrs. Shakespeare died on August 8, 1623, and that the editors had a new title printed, with the date 1623. Did they wait till she was dead before venturing to issue the volume?

Be that as it may, the folio appeared with the Droeshout engraving. Even in its best state it is such a monstrosity, that I, for one, do not believe it had any trustworthy exemplar. Those who have, as I have, examined the engraved portraits prefixed to the various collective editions of the time, will not be greatly astonished at the pretence of attaching such an abomination as the Droeshout head to the folio editions of Shakespeare.

Next in order we must place the splendid portrait, said to be by Cornelius Jansen, which passes for Shakespeare in the collection of the Duke of Somerset. Unfortunately its pedigree does not extend farther back than 1761; but Woodburn, who published in 1811 the first print from it, stated that it had belonged to Prince Rupert, who left it to his natural daughter, Mrs. Emmanuel Scroopes Howes: whence it must have come into the hands of Spackman the picture-dealer: and thence to

Mr. Jennens in 1761. The picture is of undoubted antiquity, and bears in the right hand corner, Æt. 46, 1610; which corresponds with Shakespeare's age in that year. As Jansen is known to have painted the daughter of Henry Wriothesley, Earl of Southampton, Shakespeare's friend and patron, it is not improbable that he should have painted for the earl's collection the bard himself. Then we take the Lumley, the Chandos, the Felton, the Ashbourne and the Challis portraits.

Such was our stock of the more important representations of the Bard up to about the middle of this century. Since then it has received two acquisitions, both of which were at different times in the possession of Professor Owen, at the British Museum: viz., the Duke's Theatre Bust, now in the vestibule of the Garrick Club, and the cast discovered by Ludwig Becker, now belonging to Dr. Ernest Becker, of Darmstadt. The latter professes to have been cast from a wax-mould taken from Shakespeare's face very soon after death; and I must candidly say I am not able to spot a single suspicious fact in the brief history of this most curious relic. Along with it is a miniature in oils, painted in 1637 from the cast, representing Shakespeare lying in state, his head crowned with bays.

The comparison of these various works reveals the fact that the Somerset Portrait, the Ashbourne Portrait, the Challis Portrait, and the Becker Cast, despite numberless petty discrepancies, present a substantial agreement. One can hardly doubt that they all represent one man, and that man William Shakespeare. But unfortunately for the trustworthiness of our most authentic representations there is no resemblance between any of these and either the Stratford Bust or the Droeshout engraving! In fact the former is countenanced only by the Chandos and Lumley Portraits; while the latter may have had the same original as the Felton Portrait, or the Felton may be an idealised portrait from the Droeshout.

We thus see that we have three classes of portraits: the first being led by the Stratford Bust and followed by the Lumley and the Chandos Portraits; the second led by the Droeshout engraving and followed by the Felton Portrait; or *vice versa*; while the third and by far the most interesting class is led by the Somerset Portrait and followed by the Ashbourne and the Challis Portraits, and most remarkably corroborated by the Becker Cast. How any two of these classes are to be identified I must confess myself unable to suggest. As far as I am aware no adequate experiments have been made. For one thing, I would have a plaster bust modelled after the Becker Cast; I would restore this, then vulgarise it, till I had got a poor insipid thing, such as is the Stratford Bust; I would then break off the end of the nose, and elongate the upper-lip: and I should then see whether the outcome was anything like that Bust. A great many different experiments of the sort might be suggested; but the fact that most of these relics are in private collections, and some hardly accessible, renders the task of tentative experiment both costly and difficult.

I have now to mention the various attempts that have been made in recent times to construct a trustworthy and satisfactory portrait or bust of Shakespeare. The more important of the earlier idealised portraits are the Becker Miniature, Sir Godfrey Kneller's Portrait after the Chandos, presented by that artist to Dryden, Sir Joshua Reynolds' Portrait after the same, painted for Bishop Newton, and the Hunt Portrait, now in the ante-room of Shakespeare's birth-room at Stratford. The last is believed to have been taken from the Stratford Bust, probably for something connected with the Stratford Jubilee. If so, it is singular that the nose of the bust, which is fairly arched, is not reproduced in the painting. It is, however, a very pleasing portrait; and its benignity and intelligence are very poorly represented in any of the photographic prints taken from it that I have seen. The one in Mr. J. Hain Friswell's *Life Portraits* has most unfortunately curtailed the magnificent forehead of the original. To these we must add Schemaker's Statue in Westminster Abbey and Roubiliac's Statuette, modelled for Garrick. The last furnishes the bust of our image-makers.

It is remarkable, but a fact, that the Tercentenary of Shakespeare's birth produced no work of art, either portrait or bust, which deserves mention here: nor since that time has anything of the kind been attempted in England, save Mr. Armistead's *relievo* of Shakespeare on the east side of the Albert Memorial.* America, however, is favourably contrasted with England in this particular. The Americans had many years ago testified to their enthusiasm for Shakespeare

---

* Another statue has since been placed in Leicester Square. It appears to be taken from Schemaker's.

by producing a fine bust of him, modelled by Mr. Greenough after the Caen Portrait, which had been discovered by one Mr. Joy, and brought by him to Boston. Since that time their appreciation of Shakespeare's genius, and their interest in all that concerns him, have been continually on the increase. In April, 1872, a bronze statue, executed by Mr. J. Q. A. Ward, an eminent American sculptor, was placed in Central Park, New York, and inaugurated with the usual ceremonies of unveiling and speech-making. From that time to the present this work has been a constant subject of controversy. On receiving a photograph of it from a friend in Philadelphia I was at once struck with its feebleness and untruth. It suggested to me a stern philosophic student, and certainly not a man of acute observation, ready wit and hilarious temperament. Its faults are so admirably summed up by a writer in *Lippincott's Magazine* that I offer no apology for making the following extract from his article. Mr. William R. O'Donovan writes :—

> The ideal in art, simply stated, means the portrayal of certain things in nature, giving due prominence to the characteristics in the order of their importance. Applying this proposition to Sculpture, a portrait-statue of Shakespeare should be a just expression of his individuality, based upon such portraits of him as exist.   *   *   *   Beginning with the head of the statue, the first thing that strikes one is the facial angle, which instead of approximating to the perpendicular line which distinguishes the highest Caucasian type, slopes backward, giving the angle of the lower races. A line drawn from the tube of the ear to the point of the chin will be found longer than one drawn from the same point to the prominence of the frontal bone, thus giving undue importance to the masticating apparatus, the teeth and jaws, which not only detracts from

the dignity of the head, but at once precludes all possibility of its expressing intellectuality. * * * Again, the head of the statue, as viewed from the front, * * is a compressed head, somewhat less than the usual width, and from the angle of the lower jaw to the parietal bone the line is almost straight, giving an insipidity of expression. * * The artist has modeled one side of the face from the other, making them as near alike as he could, thus [violating a great principle of nature and] departing from a most noticeable feature in the mask, &c.

and the writer shows how utterly untrue to the principal guides (the Stratford Bust, the Becker Mask, &c.) is Mr. Ward's work. He then attacks the poise of the figure, the trunk and the legs; and after some columns of very trenchant but just criticism, he closes with this peroration :

Shakespeare divined alike the motives of the boor and the king, the tenderest emotions of the most fragrant womanhood and the profoundest depths of sensuousness. As he was the greatest of poets, we may well believe him to have been the manliest of men, serene and gentle in conscious power, and thoroughly human, with inclinations as deep and varied as his thoughts. Let the reader filled with such impressions turn to this poor image and seek for one responsive thought. The opposite of every quality of Shakespeare will be suggested—first effort, the Philosopher, not the Poet, reason, not song ; then self-assertion, rather than conscious power. The head is bowed in contemplation, as if the mind were digesting something just read ; the mouth is compressed and the eyes are distended ; in every part of the figure there is exaggeration and effort without definite purpose.

Such is Mr. O'Donovan's judgment on the first statue of Shakespeare attempted in America : and so far as the photograph enables me to appreciate the various points he discusses, it seems to me a dispassionate and objective judgment.

The last contribution to the portraiture of Shakespeare

which I shall bring before you is also American: this is the so-called American Mask, being an integration of the Becker Mask, by Mr. William Page of New York. I subjoin an account of it which was published in *The New York Herald* and several other American journals of the time.

Over two years ago a distinguished gentleman called upon Mr. William Page, the artist, to ask him to paint a picture of Shakespeare. Upon consenting to perform such a task, Mr. Page had only in mind such materials as the Droeshout print, the Chandos portrait and the Stratford bust afforded for the composition of the work.

Finding, afterwards, that Messrs. J. Q. A. Ward and Launt Thompson, the sculptors, had each a photograph of a certain mask of Shakespeare, which was an object of some speculation to them just then, on account of their joint competition in furnishing a model for the statue of Shakespeare to be erected in the Central Park, he visited their studios and examined what was indeed to him a revelation. Both his brother artists asserted they had not sufficient data to settle the authenticity of the mask. Mr. Ward had availed himself of his photograph to a certain extent in the beginning, but later, feeling uncertain respecting it, he laid it aside, long before his model was perfected.

Finishing his picture for the gentleman mentioned, which the latter wished to have approximated in the general character to the Chandos portrait, Mr. Page commenced the *magnum opus* of his life. He soon obtained from England some twelve or thirteen different views of the Mask, a photograph of the Chandos as made by the Arundel Society, and the information concerning Becker's discovery, &c., which has already been set forth. When he had fairly entered upon his work, the whole matter seemed more and more plausible — the authenticity of the mask, its resemblance to the Droeshout, the Chandos and the Stratford bust. It was no easy process to properly fill up cavity after cavity from which the original pieces were wanting in the Becker Mask and still preserve or rather revive them in his own. Had Becker's Mask happily occupied his studio then, much of this trouble might have been obviated and the opportunity of terminating his labor at an earlier day been given him. It was left for him to overcome these difficulties.

* * * * * * * *

The American Mask is about two feet long, and were a figure of proportionate size made for it the whole would stand seventeen feet high. Never was there so wonderfully expressive and majestic a face as this. In it nothing is omitted; nothing is made out by negation. The veins, the wrinkles in the skin, the indications of the muscles under the skin, the smallest part recognizable to the naked eye, are given there with the same ease and exactness, with the same prominence and the same subordination, as they would be cast from nature—*i. e.*, in nature itself. Alternate action and repose are admirably displayed in it. Now the lids seem about to open, the shadow of a smile appears to linger on the lips; now again the face is grave and meditative. There is a harmony, a unity of spirit, diffused throughout the wondrous mass and every part of it, which is the glory of it. It has the freedom, the variety, the stamp of nature. There is no ostentation, no stiffness, no over-labored finish. Every part is in its place and degree and put to its proper use.

It is said, that a side view recals the profile of Julius Cæsar; the front view, the countenance of Napoleon I.

As the American Mask reproduces with scrupulous nicety every detail in the original, save such as Mr. Page refers to the decomposition of the face or to accidental injury to the plaster, it exhibits, of course, the long scar on the forehead over the right eye. It has been half seriously suggested that this is the matter to which Shakespeare refers in the 112th Sonnet:

> Your love and pity doth th' impression fill
> Which vulgar scandal stampt upon my brow ;

as if the blemish had been attributed to a discreditable source, as a tavern brawl, and the bard had been thought in danger of 'gliding almost imperceptibly from the world,' like the late

Mr. Bardell in *Pickwick*. Mr. Thoms will, I doubt not, hail this discovery as fresh evidence that Shakespeare had been a soldier; and Mr. Gerald Massey will find in the Becker Mask and the 112th Sonnet the needed confirmation of his view that some lines in John Davies' *Paper's Complaint* refer to to Shakespeare. I give the lines *in extenso*, because Mr. Massey imposed on his readers a garbled version of them. (*The Secret Drama of Shakespeare's Sonnets*, &c., 1872, *Familiar Epistle* &c.)

> But, Fame reports, ther's one (forthcomming, yet)
> That's comming forth with *Notes* of better Sett;
> And of this *Nature*; Who, both can, and will
> With descant, more in tune, me fairely fill.
> And if a senselesse creature (as I am;
> And, so am made, by those whome thus I blame)
> May judgment give, from those that know it well,
> His Notes for *Arte* and Judgement do excell.
> Well fare thee man of Arte, and World of Witt,
> THAT BY SUPREMEST MERCY LIVEST YET;
> YET, DOST BUT LIVE; yet, livst thou to the end:
> But, so thou paist for Time, which thou dost spend,
> That the deere Treasure of thy precious Skills
> The World with *pleasure* and with *profitt* fills.
> Thy long-wing'd, active and ingenious *Spright*
> Is ever *Towring* to the highest height
> Of *Witt*, and *Arte*; to beautifie my face:
> So, deerely gracest life for lifes deere *Grace*.*

---

* I quote from *The Scourge of Folly*, 1620, pp. 231 & 232. The allusion is thought by Dr. Brinsley Nicholson to be to Raleigh, who was in the Tower from 1603 to 1615. The poem was first printed in 4to in 1611, and therefore too early for Cartwright. All that Mr. Massey says of it is wide of the mark. Besides omitting, without notice, some lines from the heart of his quotation, he fancies that Davies, as *Paper*, is speaking in his own proper person.

CHAPTER VI.

MATTERS PERSONAL TO SHAKESPEARE.*

TO all true lovers of Shakespeare the most glorious thing about 'the man' is that his feet of clay are hidden from us by the impenetrable cloud of ages, while his Jovine head shines for us by its own light in his deathless works.† After the lapse of two centuries and a half of gropings into the vulgar life and outward seeming of the man, it is happily quite hopeless to 'draw his frailties from their dread abode.' It is very little indeed we may be said to know of him: and the very scantiness of our knowledge becomes the occasion of a doubt, whether the man who was in real truth the author of those works could have passed away from his surroundings without leaving some traces to shew that such a genius had

---

* Part of this chapter was published in *Notes & Queries*, 5th S. i. 81.

† A most accomplished lady, who went to her longed-for rest eleven years ago, wrote me several letters on Lewes' *Life of Goethe*. In one she thus remarks on Shakespeare: 'I have oftentimes grieved that so little was known of the inner life, the daily surroundings, of our own Shakespeare; now I thank Heaven *devoutly* for all that is *untold*. We have the golden head of *our* idol; if the feet *were* of clay, let none dare to uncover them. But he could never have been like Goethe.'

lived amongst us. Chambers, in the article to which reference has been already made (p. 55), gave this doubt a better expression than it has since received from the pen of any other writer. He says:

> On the one hand, research has traced his life from the cradle to the grave, and by means of tradition, legal documents, records, and inscriptions, [has] formed a very accurate skeleton biography; while, on the other hand, with the single exception of Ben Jonson, records and [with the exception of a few anecdotes noted by Manningham and Aubrey, and later by Oldys] even traditions are silent upon his walk and conversation; and though his signature has been several times disinterred, his whole correspondence, if he ever wrote a letter, has sunk like lead beneath the dark waters of oblivion, [leaving not so much as a] sentence that might give a faint echo of *Hamlet*. Now this, to say the least, is singular to the very last degree. *The unsurpassed brilliancy of the writer throws not one single spark to make noticeable the quiet uniform mediocrity of the man. Is it more difficult to suppose that Shakespeare was not the author of the poetry ascribed to him, than to account for the fact that there is nothing in the recorded or traditionary life of Shakespeare which in any way connects the poet with the man?*

To this sort of argument Professor Hiram Corson thus replies in *The Cornell Review* (May, 1875):

> Such testimony is more abundant in the case of Shakespeare than is any similar contemporary and immediately subsequent testimony, in the case of almost any other author of the time, either in English or in European Literature, *who was not connected with state affairs.* The personal history of a mere author, with no influence at court, was not considered of sufficient importance to be recorded, in those days when the court was everything, and the individual man without adventitious recommendations nothing.

We are certainly bound to give due weight to this consideration; and if it can be shewn that Jonson, as Poet

Laureate, or as reversionary (and virtual) Master of the Revels, was (however indirectly) 'connected with public affairs,' we need not be surprised to find the main facts of his life as well known as those of Raleigh's; while the trail of the greater meteor has almost entirely faded out. But I cannot discern in Ben's status an adequate reason for this enormous difference. It is true that we owe some of the traces of his career to his relations with the powerful and great. One of his extant autographs is a letter of two folio pages addressed by him to the Earl of Salisbury; and its preservation is unquestionably due to the rank and eminence of its recipient. But Ben's situation as a suppliant from prison was not exceptional; nor did Shakespeare enjoy an immunity from those dangers which attended upon all theatrical performances. Every dramatist in those days was wont to use old examples for the representation of modern instances, and, as it were, teach a lesson in current politics by pointing the moral of an ancient story. In doing this he could not be always sure that neither the sock nor the buskin would tread upon the corns of some influential statesman or courtier. In fact, we know that Shakespeare did thus put contemporary politics on his stage; but we have not a scrap in his handwriting soliciting a favour, or suing for an indulgence. The nearest thing to a letter *from* Shakespeare which remains to us is a letter addressed *to* him by his son-in-law's father.

But in the case of Ben Jonson, there are not only many extant letters written and signed by himself, but autograph manuscripts of *The Teares of the Howers (The Twelvth Nights*

Revells), 1604, signed at the end by Ben Jonson: *The Masque of Queenes*, 1609, with his name on the title-page: *The Masque of the Metamorphosd Gipsies*, and several of his poems, are in the British Museum Old Royal Collection, 17 B. xxxi, and 18 A xlv; and Harleian Collection, 4955. Perhaps there is a reason why the original manuscript of a Masque was more likely to be preserved than that of a Play: viz., that the manager or prompter might use the latter, the actors using *plats*:* while that of the Masque would probably remain in the possession of the author, who would himself conduct the private or semi-private performance. But we should still have to answer these questions: Why should not Shakespeare have written Masques? Why should not the original of a poem by Shakespeare be preserved as we know some of Ben Jonson's were? Evidently, the discrepancy is not yet explained.

It must be observed that, in the matter of Plays, Jonson's

---

* When a play was rough-drafted it was submitted to the Master of the Revels for his censorship. He cancelled what he did not approve and wrote his directions in the margin. In compliance with these the author wrote insertions which were attached to the draft, and the whole was submitted to the censor. There is one manuscript drama extant which has been so served: viz., *Sir Thomas More* (Harleian Collection, No. 7368). The play was then copied on pasteboards for the players. These were called *plats*, or *cards*. In *Hamlet* v, 1, 'to speak by the card' (an expression misunderstood by the Johnsonian critics) means just 'to speak no more than is set down' (iii, 2). Not more than half-a-dozen original plats are extant. Three of these were fac-similied for Mr. Halliwell in 1860: viz., *The Battle of Alcazar* (attributed to Peele), *Frederick and Basilea*, and *The Dead Man's Fortune*. The last two of these plays are lost. The plat of the third contains the earliest notice of Burbage as an actor, and that of the first gives the names of some of Alleyn's company.

manuscripts have shared the same fate as Shakespeare's: but we know more about the former than the latter. We know that they were carefully guarded by their author with a view to publication, and that they were destroyed by fire in the year in which Shakespeare died.* I do not know whether the suggestion has ever been made before, but it is surely worth consideration whether Ben had not the custody of Shakespeare's manuscripts for the same purpose as his own. Whom could Shakespeare have found so fit as Jonson to be his literary executor and editor, both as the chief friend of the author and as the chief scholar of his day in dramatic literature? I am strongly persuaded of this, that, if our bard did not carry his manuscripts to New Place, he left them in London to the care of his one faithful friend. Shakespeare died April 23, 1616, O. S.: Ward, the Stratford vicar, says that he died of a fever consequent on a merry meeting and hard drinking in company with Michael Drayton and Ben Jonson: (*Diary*, arranged by Dr. Severn, 1839, p. 183). Ben was not improbably still at New Place when Shakespeare died. Now, if Shakespeare's manuscripts were then at New Place, it seems to me not unlikely that Ben took them with him to London. We have then two contingencies, in both of which he would have the custody of Shakespeare's manuscripts for editing and printing, and, if so, they were all destroyed in the fire at Ben's house. This is, in my judgment, a far more probable supposition than that of Mr. Halliwell-Phillipps, that Shakespeare's granddaughter took

---

* I state this on Gifford's authority.

them with her to the seat of her second husband, Abingdon Hall, now the property of Lord Overstone, and that they are now mouldering away behind one of the ancient oaken panels of that mansion. I do not wonder that the noble owner regards the proposed search as a wild-goose-chase comparable to that of the lamented Delia Bacon.*

Nor yet—either in manuscript or in print—do we find any mention of Shakespeare's personal appearance till we have passed out of the period of testimony into that of tradition; and in this we have but one, and that a very indefinite, note on the subject. Aubrey, to whose painstaking research we owe so much, (though he lived too late by more than half a century to have direct knowledge of any fact about Shakespeare), mentions the tradition that 'he was a handsome well-shapt man.' In the absence of any evidence whatever rebutting this tradition, we are bound to accept it. Yet, so far from doing so, the commentators have been busy at the discreditable task of manufacturing what they call 'obscure traditions,' in order to prove that Shakespeare was ill-shaped, if not ugly: and worse, they have done their utmost to detract from his fair fame, partly by reliance on unauthenticated stories of gallantry, and partly by conclusions extorted, without the least judgment or fairness, from his *Sonnets*.

To shew how easy it is to manufacture such pseudo-biography, take the so-called 'obscure traditions' of Shakespeare's lameness. In a long and elaborate article on 'Ben Jonson's Quarrel with Shakespeare,' which was published in the *North*

* *Illustrations of the Life of Shakespeare*, part i., 1874, pp. 79-80.

British Review, July, 1870, and which appears to have been claimed by the late Mr. Richard Simpson (*Notes & Queries*, 4th S. viii. 3, col. 1), it is stated, in a foot-note to p. 411, that:

> There is some obscure tradition of a defect in Shakespeare's legs, to which he is supposed to allude in the sonnet[s];

—and the writer finds an allusion to this defect in Jonson's *Poetaster*, where Chloe asks Crispinus, 'Are you a gentleman born?' and expresses satisfaction at sight of his little legs. At least, if that be not the writer's meaning, I am unable to assign a reason for the foot-note.

Now there never was any *tradition* on the subject. The first writer who makes mention of Shakspeare's lameness was Capell. He, however, takes credit to himself for the *hypothesis*, that when Shakspeare wrote, in Sonnet 37:

> So I, made lame by fortune's dearest spite, &c.

and in Sonnet 89:

> Speak of my lameness, and I straight will halt, &c.

he was signalizing his own personal defect. Waldron entertained the same opinion, and ventilated the subject in the Introduction to his Edition of Ben Jonson's *Sad Shepherd*. A correspondent of *Notes & Queries* (5th S. iii. 134), who mentions this fact, adds:

> Waldron's opinions were extensively taken up and circulated by the reviews and magazines of the period: and it was this circumstance, probably, that gave rise to the so-called 'tradition.' Waldron backed his argument by referring to the commonly received opinion that Shakspeare, as an actor, played no leading characters, confining his representations to parts requiring no activity, as the ghost in *Hamlet*, Adam in *As You Like It*,

and kings in general. Upon the tradition that Shakspeare played Adam he laid great stress, since Adam (he says) was manifestly lame :

> 'There is a poor old man
> Who after me hath many a weary step
> Limp'd in pure love.'

After Waldron the hypothesis met with little notice and no entertainment. Malone, however, speaks of it thus :

A late editor, Mr. Capell, &c., conjectured that Shakspeare was literally lame; but the expression appears only to have been figurative. So again in *Coriolanus* :

> —— I cannot help it now,
> Unless by using means I lame the foot
> Of our design.

Again in *As You Like It* :

> Which I did store to be my foster-nurse,
> When service should in my old limbs lie lame.

In the 89th Sonnet the poet speaks of his friends imputing a fault to him of which he was not guilty, and yet he says, he would acknowledge it; so (he adds) were he to be described as lame, however untruly, yet rather than his friend should appear in the wrong, he would immediately halt. If Shakspeare was in truth lame, he had it not in his power to *halt occasionally* for this or any other purpose. The defect must have been fixed and permanent.

So far Malone. From the time when Malone's common-sense note appeared in the *variorum* edition of 1821, (vol. xx. p. 261), Capell's ridiculous fancy met with no countenance. Some fifteen years later, however, my late friend, the Rev. Wm. Harness, the Editor of Shakespeare, took up the neglected crotchet, and gave it careful nursing. In his *Life of Shakespeare* he re-states the hypothesis *as a fact*, but without any mention of its author! Mr. Harness's remarks consist mainly of an answer to Malone. 'It appears,' he writes, 'from two places in his *Sonnets* that he was lamed by accident.' He then quotes the two lines from the Sonnets, and thus proceeds:

> This imperfection would necessarily have rendered him unfit to appear as the representative of any characters of youthful ardour in which rapidity of movement or violence of exertion was demanded ; and would oblige him to apply his powers to such parts as were compatible with his measured and impeded action. Malone has most inefficiently attempted to explain away the palpable meaning of the above lines. . . . . Surely many an infirmity of the kind may be skilfully concealed ; or only become visible in the moments of hurried movement. Either Sir Walter Scott or Lord Byron might, without any impropriety, have written the verses in question. They would have been applicable to either of them. Indeed the lameness of Lord Byron was exactly such as Shakespeare's might have been ; and I remember as a boy that he selected those speeches for declamation which would not constrain him to the use of such exertions as might obtrude the defect of his person into notice.

Curiously enough, the biographer himself was, during the years of my acquaintance with him, too lame for the dissimulation which he imagined to have afforded Shakspeare a valuable resource. Mr. Harness having thus converted the foolish conjecture into a fact, it became a current remark, that our three greatest poets were afflicted with lameness!

In 1859, Mr. W. J. Thoms added his little quota to float the tradition. In *Notes & Queries* (2nd S. vii. 333) he suggested that Shakspeare's lameness might have been occasioned by his soldiering :

> The accident may well have happened to him while sharing in some of those encounters from witnessing which, as I believe, he acquired that knowledge of military matters of which his writings contain such abundant evidence.

By this time the myth had germinated, and was ready for use by any forger of Shakspeare-biography; and thus it became 'an obscure tradition.' After all, the 'obscure tradition' turns out to be so obscure as never to have existed; the whole truth being that the notion of Shakspeare's lameness was a conjecture of the eighth editor of his works, based upon a most absurd and improbable interpretation of the 37th and 89th Sonnets.

I am aware that critics of our own day are not at one as to the meaning of 'lame' and 'lameness' in these Sonnets. In any interpretation we ought to bear in mind that 'lame' had then a much wider sense than the word has now. In Jonson's *New Inn*, iv. 3, we read:

> So pure, so perfect; as the frame
> Of all the universe was lame:

where 'lame' seems to mean simply *out of gear*. For one thing; it would have been much easier for Shakespeare, if he were not lame, to simulate lameness than, if he were lame, to 'skilfully conceal' it. For my own part, I have not a shadow of doubt that 'lame' is used metaphorically in Sonnet 37: and everyone ought to see that 'lameness' in Sonnet 89 cannot be taken literally without making nonsense of the line in which it occurs.

It has been reserved for me to inform the world that Shakspeare was *crook-backed*, for has he not written, in Sonnet 90, the line:

> Join with the spite of fortune, make me *bow*?

By Fortune's spite, then, he was a hunch-back, and by Fortune's dearest spite, he was a limper! It has been recently discovered in America that Shakspeare had a scar over the left eye, to which he alludes in the same Sonnet: and his ghost appeared thrice to a Stratford gentleman, exhibiting the newly-made gash on the forehead!* So it is plain we shall have to construct a new Shakspeare, who shall be halt, hunch-backed, and scarred, like his own Richard III.

* *Birmingham Daily Mail*, Jan. 9, 1874.

Intercalary Notes.

—o—

P. 8.—With this list of sixty-four forms of our bard's surname may be compared the following fifty-seven modes in which our Scandinavian friends spell Ipswich. They are taken from the envelopes of letters addressed to Mr. C. T. Townsend, the Danish and Norwegian Consul there.

> Elsfleth, Epshoics, Epshvidts, Epsids, Epsig, Epsvet, Epsvidts, Epwich, Evswig, Exwig, Hoispis, Hvisspys, Ibsvi, Ibsvig, Ibsvithse, Ibwich, Ibwigth, Iepsich, Ie yis Wich, Igswield, Igswig, Igswjigh, Ipesvivk, Ipis Wug, Ips Witis, Ipsiwisch, Ipsovich, Ipsveten, Ipsvick, Ipsvics, Ipsvids, Ipsvidts, Ipsvig, Ipsvikh, Ipsvits, Ipsvitx, Ipsvoigh, Ipswch, Ipsweich, Ipswgs, Ipswiche, Ipswick, Ipswict, Ipswiech, Ipswig, Ipswigh, Ipswight, Ipswish, Ipswith, Ipswitz, Ispich, Ispovich, Ispwich, Ixvig, Iysuich, Uibsvich, and Vittspits.

P. 11. The orthography Shakespeare does, in fact, represent (in the spelling of the time) the received etymology. Dr. R. G. Latham retrenches the e final in his admirable *Dictionary*; for which he gave me his reason, viz., that we do not write *spear* with the e final: he having no more doubt as to the etymology *shake* (vibro) and *spear* (hasta) than other philologers —always saving Drs. Charnock and Mackay, and a few other paradoxers. The Georgian editors and commentators adopted the same spelling on the same ground; most, however, omitting the first e as well as the last. Godwin, who omits the latter e only, thus justifies the procedure:

> A frivolous dispute has been raised respecting the proper way of spelling the name of our great dramatic poet. His own orthography in this point seems to have been unsettled. Perhaps, when the etymology of a proper name is obvious, it becomes right in us to supersede the fancy of the individual, and to follow a less capricious and more infallible guide.
>
> Preface (p. iii) to Godwin's *Life of Chaucer*, 1804 (second edition).

P. 14. Shakeshaft is the name of a publican at Latchford near Warrington, and Wagstaffe was the name of several well-known writers of the seventeenth and eighteenth centuries. On the south side of Broad Street, Birmingham, we find both Wagstaff and Breakspear. There are many

Longstaffs and Shakespeares. The most distinguished of the latter name is Mr. William Shakespeare, an eminent musician and contrapuntist. Since writing my second chapter I have observed some pertinent remarks by Professor J. R. Lowell (*My Study Windows*, Sampson Low, 1871, p. 262). He writes:

"*Fautre* (sometimes *faltre* or *feutre*) means in old French the *rest* of a lance. Thus in the *Roman du Renart* (26517):

Et mist sa lance sor le *fautre*.

But it also meant a peculiar *kind* of rest. In Sir F. Madden's edition of *Gawayne* we read:

They *fentred* their lances, these knyghtes good;

and in the same editor's *William and the Werwolf*:

With sper fastened in *feuter*, him for to spille.

In a note on the latter passage Sir F. Madden says, 'There seems no reason, however, why it [*feuter*] should not mean the rest attached to the armour.' But Roquefort was certainly right in calling it a 'garniture d'une selle pour tenir la lance.' A spear fastened to the saddle gave more deadly weight to the blow. The '*him for to spille*' implies this. So in *Merlin* (E. E. Text Soc., p. 488): 'Than thei toke speres grete and rude, and putte hem in *fewtre*, and that is the grettest crewelte that oon may do, ffor turnement oweth to be with-oute felonye, and they meved to smyte hem as in mortall werre.' The context shows that the *fewtre* turned sport into earnest. A citation in Raynouard's *Lexique Roman* (though wrongly explained by him) directed us to a passage which proves that this particular kind of rest for the lance was attached to the saddle, in order to render the blow heavier:—

Lances à [lege *as*] *arçons* afeutrées
Pour plus de dures collées rendre.

Branche des Royaux Lignages, 4514-15."

P. 30, foot-note. This discussion was reported in the *Birmingham Daily Press* of Tuesday, March 3, 1856.

P. 48, foot-note. Since this chapter was printed I have received the proof-sheets of Miss Jane Lee's paper "On the Authorship of the Second and Third Parts of Henry VI, and their originals;" read at a meeting of the New Shakspere Society, October 13, 1876. It does not add much to what we already know, but is a useful summary of what has been written on the subject.

P. 55, line 22. 'There were probably sceptics of this sort before 1852.' Singer refers to a paper in the *Monthly Review*, vol. lxxxix, p. 361, &c., and vol. xciii, p. 61, &c., in which an attempt is made to show that Marlow and Shakspeare may have been one and the same person. 'This paradox is sustained,' he says, 'by some very specious arguments.'

Preface to Singer's Edition *Hero and Leander*, 1821, p. xiii.

I note also (in respect to p. 63, line 21) that in this Preface Singer does quote from p. 280 of Meres' *Palladis Tamia*.

P. 60. Chapman employs the same image in his *Monsieur D'Olive*, iv. 1 :

> What is the opinion of the many-headed Be[a]st touching my new adition of Honour?

The many-headed beast is, of course, Hydra.

> The common sort, the Hydra multitude.—Ariosto's *Seven Planets Governing Italic*, 4to, 1611.

Hydra is similarly used by Shakespeare in *Henry V*, i. 1, and in *Coriolanus*, iii. 1.

P. 69, foot-note. The reader is referred to some notes on the subject of 'the Inadequate Powers of Portraiture' in *Notes & Queries*, 5th S. iv. 363, 416, 496 ; v. 238, 497 ; vi. 276. The samples there cited thoroughly establish the position, that Ben Jonson's five couplets prefixed to the Droeshout print of Shakespeare were purely conventional, and ought not to be taken as conveying Ben's approbation of the portrait.

P. 73, l. 1. The original title of this paper was 'On some *recent contributions* to the Portraiture of Shakespeare.' Hence the force of the opening sentence.

P. 93. Since this paper was read to the Royal Society of Literature, Mr. Page has executed a bust of Shakespeare from the Becker Mask. If I may judge from the two photographs of it that I have seen, I must candidly own I do not think it worthy of either poet or sculptor.

There is also a plaster bust after the Becker Mask by Hermann Linde, which, to judge from a photograph, seems a work of merit.

P. 100, l. 23. Lameness has been imputed to Marlow also, and on utterly untrustworthy evidence.

I take this opportunity of notifying the following corrections of the text:

P. 1, l. 5, for "), p. 281," read ", p. 281)."
P. 7, l. 16, dele "(?)" and add "Shakspire," and "Shakespeare."
P. 15, l. 3, for "fewtar's" read "fewtars."
P. 39, l. 15, for "Garrick's" read "Townley's."
P. 52, second foot-note, for "a player" read "an Actor."
P. 57, penult. l. of foot-note, dele the first "1875."
P. 64, foot-note, for "more" read "most."
P. 76, l. 20, prefix "such" to "optical."
P. 80, l. 18, for "he" read "they."
P. 86, ll. 16 and 28, for "Schemaker's" read "Scheemakers'."
P. 87, l. 7, for "was" read "has been."

CHAPTER VII.

THE MODERN PROMETHEUS.[*]

εἴρχ'ηθ', οἵαις αἰκίαισιν
διακναιόμενος τὸν μυριετῆ
χρόνον ἀθλεύσω·
Prometheus Vinctus, 93—95.

EVEN the few who care for both the *integrity* and the *preservation* of Shakespeare's works will form but a very faint notion of the subject of this preliminary[†] essay from the motto. What can be the outrage which threatens either the one or the other? Are not his works, like 'the lexicons of ancient tongues,' 'comprised in a few volumes,' of which millions of copies exist? Yes, indeed; but are they 'immutably fixed?' Nay, more, is it at all likely that they will be immutably fixed? That is the doubt which suggested the following remarks. The works of Shakespeare were manifestly written to serve his own personal ends, or at

---

[*] Prefixed as a 'Justification of the Motto,' to *The Still Lion*.

[†] The essay was originally printed in *The Birmingham Gazette*, June, 1867, and subsequently prefixed to the first separate edition of *The Still Lion*, 1874. In its present place it is preliminary to the essays which constitute *Shakespeare the Book*.

most to serve the narrow ends of his own generation; and, yet, in a higher sense, they were written for all time — to subserve the pleasure and profit of ages to come. Ben Jonson summed this up in the famous line—much staled, and generally misquoted—

He was not of an age, but for all time.

Now Jonson meant to say of Shakespeare, that he *was* both *for* an age and *for* all time, which the line as it is often misquoted is made to contradict,* but also that he was not *of* an age; meaning thereby that, unlike his compeers, he was unconventional and catholic. We have a proverbial saying, 'He is a nice man *for* a small tea-party'—exquisite expansion of the *petit maître!* A man may be that without being *of* the tea-party; he may likewise be *of* the tea-party without being that. The early Christians were exhorted to be *in* the world, not *of* the world. St. Paul, for example, was not *of* the world; yet he was *for* the world; and many a man *of* the world lives *for* himself and not *for* the world. Things more distinct than *of* and *for* it were hard to find. Shakespeare was in the world of his own day; but he was not of it: he lived in an intellectual sphere above it, and so lived and wrote for it and for all time.

Even we of the nineteenth century, or fourth A.S., *know* very little what will be. We have great faith in the destiny of

---

* The most inexcusable case is that of Mr. John Leighton's 'Official Seal for the National Shakespeare Committee of 1864,' the scroll at the base of which bears the misquotation—

Not for an age, but for all time:

Shakespeare's works, and *believe* that, if they are preserved entire, they will be a most important element among those forces which go to mould the English of the future; and that what Æschylus is to us Shakespeare will be to those who speak a tongue as yet unknown, when the English of Shakespeare is bound in death.

A living language is like the mythic Proteus. It is a fluxion: no photography is swift and sharp enough to catch and arrest any one of its infinite and infinitesimal phases. But as in the old fable Proteus caught basking on the sea-shore became oracular, so when at last a language dies it not only becomes a dry logical instrument, but an oracle revealing the history of a people long after every material trace of their existence has vanished from the earth. (*Englishman's Magazine*, vol. i., p. 49; January, 1865.)

The language we speak and write is not perfectly identical with that employed by Shakespeare. English speech has moved on, and is still moving on towards the goal; and in a period which is incalculable, not for its length, but for want of exact *data*, it will be as dead as Zend, Sanscrit, Greek, or Latin. It is of no use lamenting this destiny, for it is inevitable. By no other course can a language attain to the rank of a classic tongue. Happily, when a language is dead its literature may survive. How many literatures have been swallowed up already is only known to the Creator of their creators. To deal with two only of those languages, we have reason to be thankful that the sentence executed on Hebrew and Greek spared so large and so grand a fraction of their literatures as Job, David, Isaiah,

Ezekiel, Jeremiah, Homer, Æschylus, Sophocles, Euripides, Aristophanes!

Æschylus had a narrow escape. He was judged an immortal before his death. The late Mr. Charles Knight thought Shakespeare was judged so too; but we doubt if all the evidences that can be gathered from the literatures of the sixteenth and seventeenth centuries would prove that he was thought essentially superior to Marlow, Chapman, Jonson, Beaumont or Fletcher—all men *of the age*. Even the most illiterate Greeks who were privileged to live and move in the Athens of Pericles knew that they had a demi-god among them. Every soul in that mighty auditory knew that his Æschylus 'was not of an age, but for all time.' Nay, more; Æschylus was twice as industrious a writer as Shakespeare. He created, and published in that vast arena, where from twenty to thirty thousand persons were always found to enjoy a foretaste of immortality, *twice* as many tragedies as Shakespeare wrote plays. Above seventy dramas were the pledges of their writer's earthly immortality: yet only seven survive. When the first Alexandrine Library was burnt it is said that nearly seventy single exemplars of his tragedies perished. Happily for us the immortality of Æschylus was guaranteed by the fact that imperfect copies of seven dramas existed in other libraries. Had they been perfect our Greek scholarship would have been more imperfect; for nothing short of imperfection in *such* works could have called into healthy activity the powers of our best Grecians. But only think what a narrow escape this great writer had! But for the extant seven, we could have known nothing of him at first hand. At most we might have known that the great Sophocles had a contemporary greater than himself; but we could have had no sufficient evidence to estimate the majesty and sublimity of him whose works had fallen a victim to the ambition of Cæsar.

Now, against such a catastrophe as that, Shakespeare is amply secured. Thank God, there are no single exemplars of any work of his. Compared with the great Greek his works are not so vast—thirty-seven plays, two long poems, a noble collection of sonnets, and a small volume of 'Remains,' constitute our whole stock-in-trade. But of the existing exemplars of each work the name is Legion! At any price from 1s. up to £100 the book-fancier may appropriate a complete copy of Shakespeare's works. The fount is open to all: come, all ye thirsty souls—be ye prince, poet, gentleman, artisan, labourer, tramp, or what not, here's the work for your money. Here are Warne's Chandos edition, 8vo, in boards, for 1s.; Dicks's edition, 8vo, stitched, for 1s., and in boards for 2s.; Lenny's edition, 12mo, for 2s. 6d., or, if you can afford another 6d., here is Keightley's smaller edition, 12mo and the Blackfriars edition, 8vo. You had better pay 3s. 6d., and then you may have a better choice: the Globe edition, 8vo, Mrs. Cowden Clarke's edition, 8vo or Lenny's selected edition, 12mo. Besides these there is Gray Bell's edition, 8vo, 3s. 10d., which is now reduced; and when you get up to 4s. or 5s. you may have the pick of a score of one-volume editions, and so forth, till we mount up to those costly monuments of human enterprise, Boydell's illustrated edition and Mr. Halliwell's folio edition, and lastly the original First Folio edition, accessible only to princes and merchant-princes. A thousand Alexandrine conflagrations would not at this present time burn up Shakespeare.

No! It is from no such danger that we have to rescue Shakespeare; it is from a destruction now in progress, and the cause is latent, insidious, slow and sure. The mere destruction of copies is more than compensated by new impressions; but it is precisely because there is this succession, this constant and unstaying process of supplantation and substitution, that the immortality of Shakespeare is in jeopardy. If this cause shall continue, it is demonstrable that Shakespeare's immortality can be guaranteed by only one event—the continued practice of reprinting verbatim the First Folio edition. It makes one tremble to think that but for photography there was a bare possibility (perhaps a very small one) of Shakespeare faring like Æschylus. It is almost certain that after the lapse of ages every copy which was in existence in the sixteenth, seventeenth, eighteenth and nineteenth centuries, and all which are now extant, will be utterly destroyed. We say Shakespeare's immortality is only guaranteed by the multiplication of copies. Now, from what exemplars are they made? There is a cause of corruption, constantly in operation, which must sooner or later revolutionize the whole text, viz., the practice of modernizing the old language, so as to bring it down to the standard of the English of three hundred years later. Where is this to stop? Clearly, nowhere. Language finds no arrest; it must grow or die. The innocent-looking little modifications which we now introduce into Shakespeare on the plea of textual misprinting will sooner or later themselves require modernizing. No part of the text is safe against these well-intentioned perversions; and in the meanwhile what becomes of Shakespeare? The one fact which bids fair to secure him against this fate is the multiplication of copies by photography from the folio of 1623. There is no one deed in the history of Shakespeare-literature which deserves more thanks than the recent fac-simile reprint of the first folio edition by the photolithographic process. Few know (as the writer of this volume does) the stupendous difficulties under which the first promoter of that great undertaking laboured. It would be easy to name several gentlemen who were employed in the various departments of that reproduction, to all of whom the greatest credit is due for the conscientious discharge of their several tasks; but when the history of that reprint shall be written, as written it will be, who will stand out as the originator and the finisher of the work? One there was who, at first with little aid and no sympathy, originated that reprint, and after infinite labour, miscarriage, vexation and loss, as well of health as of capital, succeeded in carrying it to a successful issue; and his name is HOWARD STAUNTON.

To his indefatigable and persistent exertions is it mainly due that Shakespeare is delivered from one source of destruction. One shoal is weathered: another is imminent; but it is one that can only acquire importance in the event of Mr. Staunton suffering a final check-mate in this new chess-game, *i. e.*, in the event of all *verbatim* reprints of the first folio being destroyed.* This source of destruction is contingent only; but whatever it is let us diagnose it. It is here that Shakespeare appears in the character of the modern Prometheus. He has committed the heinous offence of endowing men with the πυρὸς σέλας of heaven, the blaze of the fire of genius. For this the Olympian Sire, who seems to represent Persistent Conventionality, is angry, and he sends down on the Bard two ministers of vengeance. The destinies of Literature are committed to certain publishing coteries; these rule the Reviews; and the Reviews forge the thunderbolts of criticism, which at one time wound a Byron or a Shelley, and at another kill a Keats; or pour the vials of vengeance on an offending party; as once on the so-called Lake Poets. The mischief is, that *Freedom* and *Power*, the attributes of Zeus, belong (for a time) to those who have not the genius to appreciate the philosophy of mind and language, and thus *to integrate the fluxion of written speech*. Accordingly these Procrustean censors have determined, and seem determined to determine to all eternity, that the text of Shakespeare shall be measured by a standard which is hardly adequate to the criticism of Tennyson or Robert Browning. The English of Shakespeare in ten thousand places is not what now passes for good English; therefore, say the censors, it must be made good English. In a small

* Our friend suffered another kind of 'final check-mate' during the printing of this work. He died on June 22nd, 1874. Against the other Messrs. Chatto and Windus have guaranteed us by the issue of a reduced reproduction of Mr. Staunton's Folio: 1876, price 8s. 6d. Prefixed to it is a very accurate and lucid account of the First Folio, from the pen of Mr. J. O. Halliwell Phillipps. But why is Mr. Staunton not mentioned?

percentage of cases they allow the possibility of an obsolete phraseology; but not at all as to the mass. Where they do not and cannot understand him he is assumed to have fallen a prey to his own impetuosity or carelessness, or to the blundering of a compositor, and it is their task to set him right. The sluice is thus opened, and Shakespeare's language is inundated with words and phrases, some of which, indeed, he might have used; but, so far as we know, did not use: the poetry and special sense are concurrently eliminated in every spot where the critic sets his mark; and instead of 'the text of Shakespeare,' England prints and publishes 'the text of Shakespeare *restored.*' *Restored!* The very word suggests a similar process applied to architecture: indeed, the modern mode of restoring Shakespeare cannot be better illustrated than by comparing him to such an edifice as Beverley Minster: where not only is something put in the place of what has fallen a victim to time and chance, but much of what remains of the old work is ruthlessly removed to make room for an imitation of the old work by some village stonemason, who has no knowledge of or feeling for his business.

But the parallel between Shakespeare and Prometheus may be worked out in greater detail. One motive to the persecution of greatness is the jealousy of excellence, a sentiment which is begot between the Sense of Inferiority and the Love of Power. To be confronted with an author whose works have stimulated in his admirers for eight or nine generations a passion of gratitude and worship, and to find his works strange and uncouth, his phrases unusual (if not unintelligible) and his allusions obscure, is to suffer humiliation. The critic of conscious intellect and learning is offended that Shakespeare should have won a world of worshippers by works which he finds but imperfectly intelligible. He naturally seeks to disabuse those worshippers, to convict them of Fetish-worship and to bring down their idol to their own level. He will at least show them *who* is a power in the world; he will explain and correct this writer and banish to the limbo of oblivion whatever he cannot understand. As to the unfathomable, which some believe to be in Shakespeare, he says, 'Away with it to the unfathomable abyss—like to like!' All the while the critic is getting by a side wind a considerable reputation for his disinterested, courageous, and sensible conduct. This battered idol is all very well for Buddha; but he is very ugly, and (by your leave) the artist shall mend his nose and transport him to the back garden. Or the Olympian plan shall be tried, which is preferable on the whole, seeing that (as Oceanus says to Prometheus) it is not profitable to kick against the pricks,* for in the world of letters the press is exposed to the goad of public opinion, and that Shakespeare is a demi-god and was an inspired poet, is a part of its creed. It is to be acknowledged, then, that this Promethean Shakespeare is a god; he had, it is allowed, great genius and power; he did give you fire from heaven and teach

---

* This expression, which occurs in the account of the Conversion of St. Paul (*Acts* ix, 5), is nearly akin to those in the *Prometheus Vinctus* and the *Agamemnon*. It sounds strangely out of place in sequence with our Lord's declaration: for it is evident that both our Lord and the Apostle could not be at once the driver and the driven. If St. Paul were the persecutor —the 'pursuer'—it would not be in his power to 'kick against the pricks.'

you all arts. But look you, he is ungrammatical and profane, he had no knowledge of the classics, and his geography was very shaky. However, we think that much of this may have been caused by the blunders of reporters, copyists and printers. So the god is taken captive by Zeus, the public press, and handed over to the tender mercies of two emissaries, not as of old Strength and Force, but Dulness and Ignorance; and these have it in charge to manacle him hand and foot to the rock of Pedantry. But these gentlemen, though very *able* in their way, are not blacksmiths, so Hephæstus (Vulcan), the Philologer, is called in to help. A very unwilling and altogether unsympathizing agent is he. He tells them plainly, ' I really have not the heart to bind my fellow-god to this weather-beaten cliff. Yet I must on every account take heart for this business, for it is no trifle to disobey the orders of the Sire.' The prejudices of the Press infect him, and we find him clenching manacle after manacle on the suffering god; like Horne Tooke teaching us that Frenchmen are (according to Shakespeare) *brayed* in a mortar, or at least that Bertram was: (*Diversions of Purley*, 1805, ii. 50); or like Mr. F. J. Furnivall asserting that Timon's 'wappen'd widow' was merely wrapt or shrouded in her widow's weeds: (*Athenæum*, May, 1873):† with many other things quite as absurd. Philology perverted and degraded does the work of Conventionality, Dulness and Ignorance, till at last Dulness gives Prometheus a left-handed compliment to his greatness—

† We are glad to learn that our friend has withdrawn that explanation. Dr. Stratmann, however, gives the same explanation of Shakespeare's 'wappen'd widow.'

'How can mortals ever lighten thine agonies? By no true title do the divinities call thee Prometheus; *for thou thyself wilt need a Prometheus to help thee to escape this work of craft.*' How true that is! None but the man of genius can really help Shakespeare. It is only the hero who discerns, and has power to enfranchise, the hero.

The truth is, that the Sire, as the Choragus says, is administering new conventions, νεοχμοῖς νομοῖς κρατύνει and wiping out those things which men used to think great, τὰ πρὶν πελώρια ἄιστοι Here is, indeed, the gist of the crime against Shakespeare. The continual ebb and flow of language, in its growth from the conventional to the classic, is the cause of all the evil that has befallen him. It is to the strong-armed and gentle-hearted Hephæstus that we must look for help. At present he is but lame—we know who has lamed him—but sooner or later those rivets will be undone; that transfixing bolt will be withdrawn; the idiom, idiotisms and, above all, the idiasms of Shakespeare will be thoroughly understood, and so much that now goes by the board in all modern editions will be restored with intelligent reverence. This is the great work that is committed to all who have discernment or faith in the great and suffering bard.

In this case, the cause of Prometheus is the cause of our Mother Tongue. It is impossible to doubt that a great future is in store for the English language. A time must come when that language will be the language of half the world. Future literatures are bound up in its fate. Now, without exception, Shakespeare, of all who have expressed their thoughts in it, knew best how to use it. It is not from a county, a parish or a household that a language becomes enriched and defined. It is rather from the works of great popular writers. Hence it is that language acquires healthy growth and development. We can readily see, then, how large a factor in the future of English will be the works of Shakespeare, and it is now a question for us whether that factor shall be of the sixteenth and seventeenth centuries, having Shakespeare's proper impress and power, or whether it shall be a stunted and modernised Shakespeare that is to have that influence. It is now a question for us, whether we shall take side with 'the Sire' (the public critic or the press) or with Vulcan, freed from the tyranny of Zeus—whether the Promethean Bard, who has endowed us with so many heavenly gifts, shall be bound and impaled on the rock of pedantry or of conventionalism, or whether he shall be free and powerful, as he is god-like and benevolent.

I say that question is for *us*. But who are we? It is little we can do against the tyranny of 'the Sire.' We may at least do our little without fearing his censure or coveting his praise. Others may cast in their lot with him; may exalt Marlow or even Addison, and depress Shakespeare; may sneer at the Promethean fire as George III did, calling it 'poor stuff,' or scoff at Prometheus himself, as a late noble lord did, calling him 'Silly Billy.' We, for our parts, will take our stand with him against the criticasters and the detractors, and will not relax in our exertions to enfranchise Shakespeare; though it will not be our fortune to proclaim 'Prometheus Unbound:' 'for he that shall deliver is not yet.'

CHAPTER VIII.

THE IDIOSYNCRASY OF HAMLET.

IN the Tragedy of *Hamlet* we are presented with a psychological study, which has afforded delight to many an English and many a German philosopher, and which has taxed their critical powers to the utmost. The outcome of such study has been so various, and the proposed solutions of the Hamlet-problem are so discrepant, that one can only conclude that it is indeterminate, *i. e.*, admitting of more than one solution. In this chapter I do not propose to grapple with the problem as a whole, but merely to discuss one of the elements of a complete solution: viz., the peculiar idiosyncrasy of the moody Prince of Denmark.

Hamlet is introduced to us, after he has been exposed to the first disturbing influence of his life. The death of his father and the consequent marriage of his mother with his uncle have demoralised the Danish court, and Hamlet is called upon to sustain the shock of those sudden and disastrous events. We do not know what manner of man he was before calamity had marred the freshness of his youth, and driven him prematurely to take refuge in contemplation. But we do meet with him in two scenes before he is subjected to the more violent shock of the Ghost's communication; and these are for us the most important evidences of his unspoiled character.

In act i, sc. 2 and 4, we are witnesses to his conversation with the King and Queen; we hear his *first* soliloquy on suicide; and we have his first and second conversations with Horatio and the watch. On the entry of the Ghost all is changed *for* Hamlet: all is changed *with* him. Up to this point we have to gather the first *data* of the problem. With the King the prince is grimly jocular: to the Queen he is solemnly sententious: and left to himself he is the personification of melancholy. In all this we discern his dislike towards his uncle, springing from that monarch's usurpation (legal in both respects, however,) of his late brother's marital and monarchical rights. He is generous and hearty to his old schoolfellow, Horatio; he is courteous to the watch; to all—even to the despised monarch —he is the perfect gentleman. Though to himself he censures his mother for her 'wicked speed,' he is dutiful in his bearing towards her. Though to Horatio he censures his uncle for his drunkenness and his incestuous marriage, he is guarded and ceremonious in the few words (sarcastic as they are) which he addresses to the King. Beyond his kindly feeling towards all (save the usurper), and his gentlemanly demeanour, we so far see nothing especially admirable in Hamlet's character. His evident envy and his dominant melancholy are weaknesses, which, however natural to a young prince whose hopes and affections had been so early blighted, are no trustworthy guides to any of the secrets of his character. They are merely vulgar attributes. His irony and humour, which up to this point are manifested in only three brief utterances, are something more. They belong to a higher class of mind, and give the promise of genius. But, so far as we can see, there is nothing extraordinary in this young prince but his premature melancholy; and that only argues a highly sensitive organisation. So far then, we see in Hamlet a man of imagination and affection, to which early sorrow and disappointment have imparted a morbid bias. We see him first on the unfavourable side — *moody, satirical, complaining, desponding;* but the worst features of that side: his *selfishness* and *cunning:* his *procrastination* and *self-deception:* his *ribaldry* and *rant:* are not yet manifest : they all slumber there, awaiting the invocation of circumstance. It is the second shock, consequent on his first interview with his father's spirit, that brings out both his strength and his weakness.* Much in his conduct that is to us eccentric and wayward is only an incident of the nationality and period to which he belongs.

* Ophelia's estimate of Hamlet, before the advent of his troubles, must, of course, be taken *cum grano*. We must allow for the extravagance of partiality and wonderment. Her unfathomable grief was not for the loss of his love merely, but for the loss of himself : it was not so much that the Hamlet she loved had ceased to love her, but that he had been transmuted into a new person towards whom she now felt more pity than love : that a greater passion than love had cast love into the shade, and transported her lover into a new sphere. She now measured the change in him by the force of contrast impressed upon her while reeling from the shock. Accordingly, the change seemed to her immeasurable, and she portrayed his lost self in colours that were exaggerated by that force of contrast.

Apart from these, Hamlet's is just the sort of idiosyncrasy which we nowadays find so difficult to square with our conventional views of sanity. Accordingly the 'mad-doctors' find it a congenial study, and experience no difficulty in proving him to be insane. Let them once get hold of Hamlet, and there would be small fear of his troubling any king of Denmark's peace. But they overlook the *differentia* of this peculiar case, which is this: *there is no eccentricity in the Prince but what is naturally provoked by the force of circumstances.* It is not this makes a man mad, whom it does not find so. The madman forges his circumstances, or (to profit by Shakespeare's unrivalled power of expression) *imagines, or bodies forth as objects, his own incertain thought*, and then takes the false objects so imagined for real objects evoking his mental and emotional disturbance. Hamlet's case is just the reverse. A *real* ghostly visitation disturbs him, but does not unsettle or derange him. His demeanour consequent upon that visitation is only so far eccentric as the stimulus is eccentric: his eccentricity is healthy; and not to have manifested strange passion, after experiencing so strange and awful an event, would not have proved his sanity, but would have argued an insensibility and dulness comparable to that of the fat Lethean weed. Once go with the 'mad-doctors,' and assume as a *datum* of interpretation Hamlet's insanity, and his conduct becomes inexplicable, and his character more perplexing than the phenomena of storms.

But it has seemed to the critics the maddest of mad freaks for Hamlet to have assumed madness. Well, there is much to be said in excuse for this, if excuse were needed: but it is

Shakespeare, and not Hamlet, that would need the excuse, which would be found in the old romance from which the plot was derived. If further excuse be needed, I can only say I find it in the exquisite skill with which Shakespeare has grafted this incident upon a new character. An anonymous writer of 1736 thus comments on the point in question.

> To conform to the groundwork of his plot Shakespeare makes the young prince feign himself mad. I cannot but think this to be injudicious; for so far from securing himself from any violence which he feared from the usurper, it seems to have been the most likely way of getting himself confined, and consequently debarred from an opportunity of revenging his father's death, &c.

Now the King being an elected monarch could not be an usurper, and so far he could have no temptation to meddle with Hamlet. Moreover, the King was assured that Hamlet *could not* by any natural means know the fact or circumstances of his father's 'taking off.' The King, then, had no cause of fear, save on account of 'the general gender,' with whom Hamlet was a favourite, and the prince could have had no thought of 'securing himself from [his uncle's] violence.' Hamlet's motive is no secret; perhaps it is a wild enough motive: but certain it is that it was to give himself a plausible excuse for uncivil demeanour and illegal acts. It is on this score, viz., temporary derangement, that he excuses himself to Guildenstern for incivility: 'I cannot make you a wholesome answer: my wit's diseased:' and for the death of Polonius to Laertes. Somewhat after the manner of St. Paul, who argues 'So then it is no more I that do it, but sin that dwelleth in me,' Hamlet addresses Laertes thus:

> If Hamlet from himself be ta'en away,
> And, when he's not himself, does wrong Laertes,
> Then Hamlet does it not, Hamlet denies it.
> Who does it then? His madness: if't be so,
> Hamlet is of the faction that is wrong'd;

an argument which is quite worthy of the clown in the fifth act. As I read the play, this is given by Shakespeare as an example of the self-justification to which Hamlet intended, in the event of indiscretion, to put in his claim. But things turned out very different from what he expected. The error of taking Polonius for his betters and killing him like vermin frustrated all his plans, and the madness which was to have saved him harmless becomes a good reason for his removal. He learned too late the danger of deep plotting. We must, however, bear in mind that the madness assumed by Hamlet was a mere 'antic disposition,' occasionally resorted to, and least of all dreamed of when he is carried away by that passion to which the idiosyncrasy of the Dansker as well as the Norseman was peculiarly liable. It is to this Hamlet refers when he says to Laertes, at Ophelia's grave,

> I pr'ythee take thy hand from off my throat;
> For, though I am not splenetive and rash,
> Yet have I in me *something dangerous*,
> Which let thy wisdom fear.

This passion, in its more awful and destructive phases, constituted what was called the Berserkir Rage; which is well described by Sir Walter Scott in the following lines in *Harold the Dauntless*.

> Profane not youth—it is not thine,
> To judge the spirit of our line—
> The bold Berserker's rage divine,
> Through whose inspiring, deeds are wrought
> Past human strength and human thought.
> When full upon his gloomy soul
> The champion feels the influence roll,
> He swims the lake, he leaps the wall—
> Heeds not the depth, nor plumbs the fall;
> Unshielded, mailless, on he goes
> Singly against a host of foes;
> Their spears he holds like withered reeds,
> Their mail like maidens' silken weeds;
> One 'gainst a hundred will he strive,
> Take countless wounds, and yet survive.
> Then rush the eagles to his cry
> Of slaughter and of victory;
> And blood he quaffs like Odin's bowl,
> Deep drinks his sword—deep drinks his soul,
> And all that meet him in his ire
> He gives to ruin, rout, and fire;
> Then, like gorged lion, seeks some den,
> And couches till he's man agen.

Mr. Carlyle, in his *Early Kings of Norway*, thus describes the rage of the same Harold at Stamford Bridge.

Enraged at that breaking loose of his steel ring of infantry, Norse Harald [Hardrade, this time] blazed up into true Norse fury, all the old Væringer and Berserkir rage awakening in him; sprang forth into the front of the fight, and mauled, and cut, and smashed down, on both sides of him, everything he met, irresistible by any horse or man, till an arrow cut him through the windpipe, and laid him low for ever. That was the end of King Harald and of his workings in this world.

Hamlet's rage, as exhibited first, after the armed Ghost's disappearance, and last at the grave of Ophelia, is but a child's pet compared with the Berserkir Rage; and in the same proportion is the soul of Hamlet to that of a knightly Norseman. But for the visit of the Ghost, which is the instrument to try the stuff the prince is made of, he might have passed for a strong-hearted and doughty youth, in whom the hereditary rage had been subdued by knightly training. What such a true knight was, both before and after the rage had been brought into subjection, we may learn from La Motte Fouqué. In his *Theodolf* we have the Hamlet-like humour, kindliness, coolness, and energy of character, exquisitely balanced, and coexisting with the purest ethic grandeur. Here, too, the emergency arises which intensifies one pole of his character, and the current of motive is completed.* At length the one weakness in the

---

* Theodolf's Berserker rage had awoke. Once again he asked, with flashing eyes, ' Wilt thou give her to me? Is she ready to depart?' And the delay of the answer was the signal for the most fearful outbreak.

Knives and other sharp instruments, caught up at the moment by the furious Icelander, flew on all sides of the room like a shower; and many fell senseless or dead to the ground, on whose lips a bold smile yet rested. As the rest rushed in anger and terror against the raging youth, a mighty stroke of the battle-axe struck the breast of the foremost; and then the good sword Throng-piercer began its fearful meal.

It was less a fight than the annihilating wrath of nature's strength let loose against man's weakness. Soon there were only bloody corpses lying about in the hall just before so gay; and a few wounded men, with every sign of terror, were tottering down the stairs. The fearful Theodolf stood alone in the deserted blood-stained hall.   *   *   *   *   *
and he sank down among the dead in heavy exhaustion, more overcome by the weight of grief [for the loss of Isolde] than by his wounds.—*Theodolf the Icelander*. [London: Edward Lumley. 1865. P. 153.]

character of Theodolf, viz., the hereditary Berserkir Rage, is over-matched by that ethic sovereignty which wins him over to 'the White Christ.' In the case of Hamlet, as in that of Theodolf, it is the emergency that tries his mettle, and from his conduct in it may we infallibly infer his character. For another example, Fouqué's hero, Count Wildeck, is introduced to us as a worthy knight before his character is put to proof. But his courage, truth and fealty—in a word, his *virtue* or manly worth—cannot be duly estimated till his encounter with the terrible maniac in the castle of Rosaura's kinsman. Had he resorted to selfish lying or stratagem, had he been carried away by any pathological influence whatever, or, as our old writers say, 'forsaken himself,' we should have felt that his was a weak character deserving our pity if not our contempt: and that is the only alternative offered us in the case of Hamlet.

But we are not driven to have recourse to fiction to illustrate the peculiarities of Hamlet's idiosyncrasy. We are sure to find among imaginative men many examples in point: and especially among philosophic poets. Coleridge was a very different being from Hamlet: and yet he manifested in a remarkable degree the disposition to dissolve action in meditation. In fact, he himself was struck with the resemblance.* He lacked, like Hamlet, the stimulus of a healthy narrowness. Had his roots been confined to a flower-pot, his stem would have been forced

---

* 'I have a smack of Hamlet myself, if I may say so' (*Table Talk*, 1851, p. 40). This modest assertion becomes in Mr. Minto's hands a 'notion that Hamlet's character was exceedingly like his own.' *Characteristics of English Poets*, 1874, p. 279.

into flower and fruit.* As it was, his intellectual vagrancy was fatal to sustained exertion; so that much of what he attempted was but inchoate, if not abortive; and much more that he intended to accomplish never got one step beyond the intention. He whose task is coextensive with the world will hardly attempt its performance; while the restricted task which a man does achieve must be the whole world to him.

* 'As the air we breathe is not all air, and true courage has an ingredient of fear in it, the intellect should part with something of its own nature to qualify itself as proper human intellect. It should yoke itself contentedly with a wholesome narrowness, in a compound practical and intellectual being. Its largeness tends, without such check, to feebleness. The mind of Hamlet lies all abroad, like the sea—an universal reflector, but wanting the self-moving principle. Musing, reflection, and irony upon all the world, supersede action, and a task evaporates in philosophy.'—Prof. J. B. Mozley's article in the *Christian Remembrancer* (art. vii, vol. xvii, January, 1849).

On this Mr. C. J. Monro writes to me as follows:—

'I do not feel satisfied of the truth of this doctrine at all, at least as stated. Is not unhealthy width simply inadequate will? I do not mean will below the average strength, but below the strength adequate to intellect. I suppose a comprehensive intellect requires a corresponding strength of will: and the chances are that a man of extraordinary comprehensiveness would not also have an extraordinary force of will. I am supposing the two gifts to be tolerably *independent*, so that we are not obliged to suppose them *antagonistic* in order to account for the rarity of adequate force of will in men of extraordinary comprehensiveness: and surely the combination is only rare, not unknown. As to Hamlet's idiosyncrasy, there is a point which may have been often noticed, for certainly it is obvious, real or not; namely, that if thought outweighs will, speech outweighs everything else in him. In two places he shows some consciousness of being more in word than matter; as, when he checks his own protestations to Horatio with 'something too much of this,' and when he reproaches himself, at the end of a soliloquy, with unpacking his heart with words. But he shows it unconsciously and with exquisite simplicity when he admires the poor player so highly in comparison with himself, because he can *give tongue* so powerfully and all for Hecuba.'

Hamlet's generalization, which he calls 'thinking too precisely on the event,' is the inner correspondent to that analytical irony which Horatio (good, common-sense man) calls 'considering too curiously.' One might summarize the matter thus, that the irony is Hamlet's revenge for having allowed his resolution to evaporate in meditation.* He takes it out in vivisection. In this there is no little spite, and a good deal of foolishness. Hamlet is humorous, and humour is commonly a sign of intellect. The lack of humour in Milton and Tennyson is a psychological fact deserving study. But even humour is in morbid excess, if it degenerate into wanton mischief or cowardly malice. Such was the humour of Dean Swift; and in that he was much worse than Hamlet, whose malice usually stops short of malignity and evaporates in banter or mockery. It is thus that he makes his father's ghost a 'mole' and a 'pioneer,' as if he were a bodily substance, burrowing his way through the earth from place to place in suite of the watch. It is thus that he shows 'how a king may go a progress through the guts of a beggar,' viz., by the mediation of a fish that has eaten a maggot bred in the king's carcase. It is thus that he traces 'the dust of Alexander till he finds it stopping a beer-barrel' or staunching a hole in the roof. Akin to this perverse analysis is the irreverence with which he habitually treats those whose condition entitles them to the respect or the pity of their

---

* 'The lofty ruminator within exhibits himself as a jester and an oddity without; and, not content with levity, he assumes madness, as if to enable himself to enjoy a fantastic isolation from the world and human society altogether, and to live alone within himself.'—Prof. Mozley's article in the *Christian Remembrancer*.

fellows: Ophelia, a simple, trustful, fragile young creature, who had loved him and in filial duty had rejected him, is a fair mark alike for his heartless mockery and his ribald gallantry; and the superannuated old chamberlain, her father, is mocked behind his back, and twitted to his face with the infirmities of age. I am far from denying that the horrible web of crime and vice in which Hamlet found himself thus early entangled should be allowed to extenuate, if not palliate, the guilt of such conduct in a man with such predispositions: but that is because the predispositions are there.

The poet Shelley had all Hamlet's faculty of subtil analysis and more than all his poetical furor, but with little of the humour that characterizes the Dane. Accordingly we find in Shelley the same proclivity to associate objects with disgusting if not irrelevant details: *e. g.*,

> Yet not the meanest worm
> That lurks in graves and fattens on the dead
> Less shares thy eternal breath,
> Spirit of Nature!—*Queen Mab*, i.

> and on that arm [the King's]
> The worm has made his meal.—*Ibid.*, iii.

> And thou did'st laugh to hear the mother's shriek
> Of maniac gladness, as the sacred steel
> Felt cold in her torn entrails.—*Ibid.*, vi.*

---

* I once heard the reply of an accomplished man of the world to the question—'Why not call a spade a spade?' He answered—'By all means, except in cases where the common sense of the world has covered its nakedness with the garb of decency. In those cases what is to be gained by stripping it off? Why should we be ever reminded of our weaknesses and impurities? No: the advantage is all the other way.'

Lord Byron had more than all Hamlet's selfishness, moodiness, ribaldry and heartless mockery. Lord Lindsay (*The Times*, Oct, 18, 1869) thus describes him: he might have been describing Hamlet:—

> There was a waywardness in Byron's mind, a tinge, not merely of that 'madness' which is so nearly allied to 'great wit,' but of 'hereditary melancholy,' which ran, like a subtil poison, through all its mazes, and broke out alternately in self-accusation, enhanced (as in many such cases) by the pleasure of producing a sensation, and in a grim, if not ferocious, and (so to say) freakish merriment, the very reverse of romance and enthusiasm while it lasted, that may well have amazed, terrified, and disenchanted a young and inexperienced, although noble-spirited, woman like Lady Byron. This last consideration, the morbid tinge which, not amounting to insanity proper, renders such men liable to abnormal conditions of temper and conduct, subjecting them to unmerited constructions, * * * may seriously modify any conclusion come to from Lady Anne [Barnard]'s narrative.

Lady Anne Barnard thus writes of the marriage of Lord and Lady Byron.

> They had not been an hour in the carriage which conveyed them from the church when, breaking into a malignant sneer, 'Oh! what a dupe you have been to your imagination. How is it possible a woman of your sense could form the wild hope of reforming *me?* Many are the tears you will have to shed ere that plan is accomplished. It is enough for me that you are my wife for me to hate you; if you were the wife of any other man I own you might have charms,'* &c.

Many were the sallies he made on her in that spirit, some of which seemed to have vacillated between jest and earnest, and

---

* This admirative reflection strongly recalls Lamia's reply to Titus, who had been advising him to take a second wife, Domitian having appropriated the first: μὴ καὶ σὺ γαμῆσαι θέλεις;—as if the Prince himself were looking out for an *eligible* partner.

some were mere admirable acting, what he called 'philosophical experiments,' which were intended to serve no other end than to make her understand that he had mastered her, or seen through her, and despised her for her simplicity. His assumed insanity, too, is curiously illustrative of Hamlet's. 'He would then,' writes Lady Anne Barnard, 'accuse himself of being mad, and throw himself on the ground in a frenzy.' Again, 'he has wished to be thought partially deranged, or on the brink of it, to perplex observers and prevent them from tracing effects to their real causes through all the intricacies of his conduct.' In all this he over-acted the part of Hamlet, and shewed himself more selfish and malignant than the Dane; yet the two characters have many points of contact. The man of knightly breeding, while he shows no mercy to the meannesses and vices of human nature, habitually and delightedly treats its infirmities with gentleness and compassion. The pretty follies and naive mischief of the child, the weaknesses of the woman and the foibles of the old are alike the objects of his affectionate consideration. To recur once more to fiction for the illustration of this point: we may note how in De Quincey's *Avenger* it is said, that Margaret's filial tenderness for her old grandfather was not only on her dead mother's account, but that he was himself 'continually making more claims on her pity, as the decay of his memory and a childish fretfulness growing upon him from day to day marked his increasing imbecility.' Again we may call to mind that exquisite touch of knightly breeding which Mrs. Gaskell imparts to her poor farmer-lad, Will Leigh, who seeing a half-drunken old man, who was being mocked by a crowd of juvenile Hamlets for the unsteadiness of his gait, took care of him and escorted him home. 'For his [own] father's sake Will regarded old age with tenderness, even when most degraded and removed from the stern virtues which dignified that father.' (*Lizzie Leigh*, p. 10.) To such a feeling as that Hamlet is an utter stranger. As it seems to me a selfish conceit infests his every thought and action. To him an old man who had run to belly was known by the familiar *sobriquet* of 'guts,' and his shrunken, feeble legs and rheumy eyes were to him nothing but the fruits of intemperance and unchastity. For my part, I know not how any man of right feeling can find sufficient excuses for Hamlet's perverse humour, in the disappointment of his young ambition and the sensitiveness of his organisation. His temperament and his surroundings may help us to explain his eccentricities, but hardly to excuse them.

Allowing, as I do, that the excess of reflection in Hamlet was a factor in his irresolution and procrastination, there is still another factor, and one that is a special motive to that particular line of conduct which he pursued; viz., his own selfish interest. The disappointment and humiliation which he suffers in consequence of his uncle's election provoke a sentiment which has two poles: hatred of the supplanter and desire of redress. So far forth any promptings he might have to remove by violence the obstacle in the path of his ambition are neutralized by the fear of damaging his own chance of succession. Then comes the Ghost's injunction in corroboration of the former pole; and in the first passion of indignation and grief Hamlet is capable enough to execute the vengeance to which he is thus doubly incited. But, unlike the preceding motives, this added motive is liable to diminution by lapse of time. All such impressions wear away, unless renewed, as Coleridge well remarks of the terrors of a popular revolution.* The lesson, however startling, is soon forgotten. In Hamlet's case, the first impression of the Ghost's visit is strong and deep; but it soon begins to wane. Finding this to be the case, and seeking to blind himself to the fact, that his newly formed purpose is being blunted, the Prince pretends that he may be the dupe of an evil spirit: his uncle may be innocent: the Ghost may have been a messenger from hell or an infernal hallucination. 'I'll have proof more relative than this,' he exclaims. The device of the play removes the scruple, and then Hamlet tries to make himself believe that he is as hot for revenge as when the Ghost left him. 'Now could I drink hot blood.' But it is all poor acting. The second visit of the Ghost deepens the impression, which, however, is destined again to fade into insignificance. The prince's self-interest has still the ascendancy, and remains the dominant motive to the end of the play. He kills Polonius, hastily judging him to be the King, and thinking that if it were any other eavesdropper it would not much matter. Whoever it was, 'the situation would excuse the act; but he will not do it when the King is at prayers, because he fears the consequences of such an open murder.'† We may be sure he would now, without

* Coleridge's *Friend*, 1844, vol. i, p. 244.
† These are the words of Mr. A. E. Brae, in a letter to myself, dated 28th November, 1853.

any additional motive, have killed the King, if he could have done so without danger to his succession. Whatever is a bar to his self-interest or promotion is doomed to be destroyed 'with *safest* haste.' He knew, for instance, that Rosencrantz and Guildenstern were wholly innocent of participating in the design against his life: but he had the opportunity of silencing them without compromising himself, and he was not the man to let it slip: and having accomplished their destruction he does not find them near his conscience, because 'they made love to their employment.' *

* This fragment was the only written part of a dissertation originally designed for a volume of *Shakespeare Essays*, by various authors, which never saw the light.

CHAPTER IX.

SOME PASSAGES REPRIEVED.

SINCE the publication of *Shakespeare Hermeneutics* in 1875, several isolated criticisms have been brought under my notice which might well have been included in that volume. Most of these relate to passages in *A Winter's Tale* and *Cymbeline*, a pair of plays which having been written about the same time, probably in 1611, present many features in common, and aptly illustrate what we may call the *meta-climax* of Shakespeare's genius. At this time he had written his greatest comedy, *Measure for Measure*, and his five greatest tragedies, *Othello, Macbeth, Lear, Antony and Cleopatra* and *Coriolanus;* and probably also *The Tempest*, in which the signs of decadence, both in grammatical construction and in metre, are most strongly marked. The other criticisms deal with passages in *As You Like It* and *Antony and Cleopatra*. These we will dispose of first.

1.—*As You Like It*, act ii, sc. 1.

> *Duke Sen.* Now my coe-mates, and brothers in exile:
> Hath not old custome made this life more sweete
> Then that of painted pompe? Are not these woods
> More free from perill then the envious Court?
> Here feele we not the penaltie of *Adam*,
> The seasons difference, as the Icie phange
> And churlish chiding of the winter's wind,
> Which when it bites and blowes upon my body
> Even till I shrinke with cold, I smile, and say
> This is no flattery: these are counsellors
> That feelingly persuade me what I am:

On the assumption that there is no misprint in this text, three interpretations have been suggested.

1. That of Boswell (the continuator of Malone), who proposed to take *feel* in the sense of *feel injuriously* or *suffer from*: as to which it is sufficient to refer to the last line, where to 'feelingly persuade' is obviously to persuade by means so painful as to be comparable to the bite of a venomous creature: so that the Duke could not consistently say

> Here feele we not [injuriously] the penaltie of Adam

if that penalty was the vicissitudes of the seasons.

2. It has been proposed to understand by 'the penaltie of Adam,' bodily labour, but this makes nonsense of the after-passage commencing with 'the seasons difference:' besides which a passage in *Paradise Lost*, book x, line 651, and Bp. Newton's note on lines 668 *et seq.*, attest the prevalence of the old scholastic doctrine that the changes of the seasons was the immediate consequence of Adam's fall.

3. The last and most rational of the attempts which have been made to interpret the unaltered text is that of Mr. C. J. Monro, who wrote to me, under date November 17, 1874, as follows :

> All I can say is that, as it seems to me, the directest sense is got by retaining *not* and making the sentence interrogative. Interrogative—because the Duke cannot wish to affirm that they feel not, etc.: and retaining *not*—because *but* would only fit in if he wished to minimize what they feel, whereas that is not his intention in the relative words. But this only shows that you thus get the directest sense : for I cannot reconcile myself to the interrogation, because it makes the sentence an enigma for the last five lines. So if it is really true that *not* and *but* are often interchanged (at least, if *not* is often put for *but*), I should incline to Theobald's emendation. Reading *but*, I suppose the Duke to mean
>
> > 'Now that we are away from the Court, we do not feel ourselves among the perils of envy and hatred [and flattery]: we *only* feel the weakness entailed, by Adam's transgression, upon humanity, and it does one good to be made to feel *this*.'
>
> But there seems to me something too jaunty in setting out with a *but* with the sense of *only*; so I am not quite satisfied any way.

However we may regulate and interpret the passage, there is certainly a hitch; but it is to me very questionable whether the hitch be sufficiently great to justify verbal emendation. Assuredly if emendation be resorted to Theobald's conjecture is very plausible. But probably sufficient justification might be found for *now* in the place of 'not': *now* referring to the present time of winter, after which the 'penaltie' would be no longer felt?

II.—*Ibid*, act ii, sc. 6.

>   *Jaques.* . .   O that I were a foole,
> I am ambitious for a motley coat.
>   *Duke Sen.* Thou shalt have one.
>   *Jaques.* It is my only suite,
> Provided that you weed your better judgements
> Of all opinion that growes ranke in them,
> That I am wise. I must have liberty
> Withall, as large a Charter as the winde,
> To blow on whom I please, for so fooles have :
> And they that are most gauled with my folly,
> They most must laugh : And why sir must they so ?
> The why is plaine as way to Parish Church : *
> Hee, that a Foole doth very wisely hit,
> Doth, very foolishly, although he smart
> Seeme senselesse of the bob. If not,
> The Wise-man's folly is anathomiz'd
> Even by the squandering glances of the foole.
> Invest me in my motley : Give me leave
> To speake my minde, and I will through and through
> Cleanse the foule bodie of th' infected world,
> If they will patiently receive my medicine.

I here give the disputed passage with as much of the immediate context as will serve to explain it. When I gave my brief interpretation in *Shakespeare Hermeneutics*, pp. 81, 82, I was hopeful, too hopeful as the event showed, of carrying every reader with me. I must own to no little regret that such an able exponent of Shakespeare as Mr. W. Aldis Wright should find my interpretation inadmissible. (See the Clarendon

---

* Unfortunately Shakespeare's commentators have not found it so. Theobald missed the way; and all but a certain worthy named Whiter followed Theobald, and went astray.

Press Edition of *As You Like It*, pp. 115-116.) Were I engaged in the restoration of a corrupt text, I should regard the prolonged discussion of a verbal emendation as too suggestive of 'the mountain in labour.' But the defence and exposition of a passage in the Folio text stand on a very different footing; and I shall make no apology for restating the argument on which I rely for the interpretation of Jaques' speech.

The wind is the symbol of lawlessness. It blows where it listeth, and upon whom it listeth, not seldom inflicting pain with its 'icy fang and churlish chiding.' The moral of *As You Like It* is, the lesson conveyed in so many verbal forms, that such evils are but 'the penalty of Adam,' 'that feelingly persuade us what we are.'

In *Henry V*, i, 1, we read,

> When he speaks,
> The air, a chartered libertine, is still.

So Jaques asks for

> 'as large a charter as the wind,
> To blow on whom I please.'

He demands the fool's privilege of taking random shots, of uttering indiscriminate and general censure. Mr. Staunton had this passage in mind when he proposed *tax* as a substitute for *wax* in *Timon of Athens*, i, 1,

> My free drift
> Halts not particularly, but moves itself
> In a wide sea of *tax*. No level'd malice
> Infects one comma of the course I hold.

So Jaques, in his diatribe on pride of dress and the love of bravery (which follows the passage under consideration), says:

> if it [my tongue] do him right,
> Then he hath wrong'd himself: if he be free,
> Why then my *taxing* like a wild-goose flies,
> Unclaim'd of any man.

The advantage of this course is, that no one can take offence without admitting the applicability of the hit to himself.

> And they that are most galled with my folly,
> They most must laugh: And why, Sir, must they so?

Then Jaques proceeds to show 'the why.' He follows Euclid's method, in first restating the proposition in another form, and then proving it by *reductio ad absurdum*. The following is the enunciation of the proposition to be proved:

> He, that a fool doth very wisely hit,
> Doth* . . (although he smart)
> Seem senseless of the bob.

This is proved as follows:

> If not,
> The . man's folly is anatomiz'd
> Even by the squandering glances of the fool.

Which I may paraphrase in these words:

If you deny it, let us suppose that, because he smarts, he does not seem senseless of the bob, but winces under it: now he thereby shows that he

---

* This 'doth' is merely auxiliary: cf.

'Doth very foolishly seem senseless' &c.,
and   'Did coldly furnish forth the marriage tables.'

Hamlet, i, 2.

is a 'galled jade,' that one of the fool's blows has wrung him; and accordingly he is anatomized,* *i. e.*, his faults are shown up, even by the random hits of the fool. But no man in his senses would do this. Therefore etc., Q.E.D.

It will be observed that I have omitted some words in the foregoing quotations. I am sensible that I laid too great an emphasis upon 'very foolishly' and 'wise' in the brief exposition I gave in *Shakespeare Hermeneutics*, p. 81. I now see plainly that neither qualification is *essential* to the sense. The assailant being 'a fool,' the assailed is considered as 'wise.' The fool is said to hit 'very wisely' when he hits a blot,† and therefore by similar contrast the sufferer is said to act 'very foolishly.' This is perhaps all the weight we should lay on these qualifications. At the same time, it should be recognised that they will carry more. The assailed may well be called wise if he does not betray his folly by wincing under the lash. Yet, for all that, he cannot help feeling very foolish in dissembling his mortification. He is thus made to feel foolish in acting wisely, and the fool makes him act wisely by making him conscious of his folly.

* Cf. Oliver's speech to Charles in act i, sc. 1.

I speake but brotherly of him, but should I anathomize him to thee, as hee is, I must blush and weep, and thou must looke pale and wonder.

Also the following lines in Dryden's prologue to *Julius Caesar*:

Cf. Johnson with skill dissected human kind,
And shew'd their faults, that they their faults might find;
But then, as all anatomists must do,
He to the meanest of mankind did go,
And took from gibbets such as he would show.

† The more the pity, that fools may not speak *wisely* what wise men do foolishly.—*As You Like It*, i, 2.

Mr. Aldis Wright records three objections to my interpretation of this passage.

First.—'It is not said that the fool doth wisely in hitting a wise man.' I allow this and take the consequences.

Secondly.—'Dr. Ingleby's explanation would seem to require "because he smarts" instead of "although he smarts," as showing how it is that the wise man's dissimulation is foolish or awkward.' Mr. Aldis Wright here mistakes my reading of the passage. He supposes me to take 'although he smart' (not 'smarts') as qualifying 'very foolishly,' whereas I take it as qualifying 'doth seem senseless of the bob.' The wise man dissembles the smart *although* he feels it; and this, notwithstanding that he does it foolishly *because* he feels it.

Thirdly.—The reading I stand by is (in Mr. Aldis Wright's view) a mere repetition of what Jaques has just said—

> And he that is most galled with my folly
> He most must laugh.

If this objection were of the least validity it would be a ground for the emendation of every proposition in Euclid which is proved by *reductio ad absurdum:* his method being to state the proposition in its generality showing the thing to be proved; then to restate it in its application to the method of proof, and lastly, to trace the consequences of denying it. The only difference, in fact, between Euclid and Jaques lies in this, that Jaques proves the general proposition in order to substantiate a particular application of it: a difference which gives the repetition the fullest justification. In point of fact, Jaques' proof beginning 'If not' is inconsequent unless it follows the particular *affirmative* statement; and Theobald's emendation, which Mr. Aldis Wright accepts, viz.—

> Doth very foolishly although he smart,
> *Not to* seem senseless of the bob. If not, &c.

saddles the passage with a glaring solecism which we have no right to impute to Shakespeare: who, to convey the sense required by Theobald, would have written (but for the metre)

> *Would do* very foolishly, although he smart,
> Not to seem senseless of the bob. If *so*, &c.

III.—In *Antony and Cleopatra*, ii, 2, Cæsar brings a series of charges against Antony, the first of which is on this wise:

> Your wife and brother
> Made wars upon me; and their contestation
> Was theme for you, you were the word of war.

This Antony denies, and adds—

> If you'll patch a quarrel,
> As matter whole you have to make it with,
> It must not be with this.
> *Cæs.* You praise yourself
> By laying defects of judgment to me; but
> You patch'd up your excuses.

Rowe introduced the word *not* after 'you have;' and in this he was supported by Dr. Johnson, Malone and nearly all the editors: and all modern editions read

> As matter whole you have not to make it with.

The words, as they stand in the Folio,

> As matter whole you have to make it with,

admit of grammatical analysis in two ways: either 'matter whole' is the objective governed by 'you have,' as all the editors would read it; or 'matter whole' is governed by 'with,' and 'you have' is not the verb of possession, but the verb of obligation. If Shakespeare meant, as I believe, to employ the verb *have* in the latter sense, he could not have arranged the words in any other way than that in which they have come down to us, without either misleading construction or faulty prosody.

As you have matter whole to make it with

would be misleading; for every one would make 'matter whole' the objective to 'you have:' and

As you have to make it with whole matter

would not be metrical. I observe that the use of the verb *have* in the sense of obligation is not uncommon with Shakespeare, *e. g.*,

Wishing Adonis had his team to guide. (*Venus and Adonis*, l. 179.)

i. e., wishing Adonis, instead of making love, had to look after his team.

Antony refers to former letters, and Cæsar to former excuses: so that when Antony speaks of *patching the quarrel*, he means that the quarrel has been already *worn out* by discussion. Cæsar ought (he says) to be able to adduce a new and entire ground of complaint: but that if he will patch up the old quarrel he must do it with something else than the pretence that Antony's wife and brother have made wars upon him.

It is almost impossible to anticipate and provide against all objections. I foresee one, as to the use of the conjunction 'as' in the second line. It is what I call the *conjunction of reminder*, being employed by Shakespeare and his contemporaries to introduce a subsidiary statement, qualifying, or even contradicting, what goes before, which the person addressed is required to take for granted, *e. g.*,

> Though you have no beauty,
> As by my faith I see no more in you, etc.
> *As You Like It.*

> Admit no other way to save his life,
> As I subscribe not that nor any other, etc.
> *Measure for Measure.*

> Say this becomes him,
> As his composure must be rare indeed, etc.
> *Antony and Cleopatra.*

This conclusive interpretation of the text was proposed to me by Professor Sylvester, the world-renowned mathematician. After this, an editor who shall reprint the text with Rowe's emendation will only have the excuse of ignorance.

IV.—There is a passage at the end of the first act of *A Winter's Tale* which has usually been regarded as the seat of an incurable corruption, though it has been variously tinkered with a view to its restoration. Polixenes says:

> Feare ore-shades me:
> Good Expedition be my friend, and comfort
> The gracious Queene, part of his Theame; but nothing
> Of his ill-ta'ne suspition.

So runs the text of the Folio 1623. I see no advantage in repeating the various alterations which have been suggested. Let it suffice to say that Steevens understood 'comfort' as a verb governing 'nothing,' and quotes Paulina's remark as to 'comforting his evils.' Warburton read *Queen's* for 'Queene,' meaning '[let] comfort [be] the gracious queen's [friend]:' and one of the latest critics privately proposed to me to put a point after 'comfort,' taking 'comfort' (like Warburton) as a substantive. For myself, I will not attempt to pronounce on the merit of such conjectures; for I labour under the disqualification of not being able to see in the passage anything whatsoever requiring alteration. I see in it a fine example of Shakespeare's terseness, and two archaic phrases.

1. As to the terseness of the phrase

> Good expedition be my friend, and comfort
> The gracious Queene,

surely this means 'Let both of us make *good speed*.' On this, compare the expression 'the Queen's speed' in act iii, sc. 2. The sentence may be thus paraphrased: 'Let me have good speed for my friend, and the Queen have good speed for her comfort.' Polixenes stood in pressing need of *friendly help*, to enable him to escape his enemy Leontes; and Hermione stood in special need of *comfort* to enable her in her present physical condition to sustain the troubles consequent on her husband's jealousy.

2. The one archaic phrase is *to be part of*, meaning, to contribute to. Thus, in Posthumus' soliloquy on Death in *Cymbeline*, v. 4:

> If of my freedom 'tis the main part,

i. e., if my death will mainly contribute to my freedom, &c. Compare also the King's words in *Cymbeline*, act iv, sc. 3: 'Imogen, the great part of my comfort, gone.' The king's 'theame' was of the Queen and Polixenes: each contributed to it, as he himself says in act ii, sc. 3,

> part o' the cause, [*i. e.*, of his grief]
> She, the adultress: for the harlot king
> Is quite beyond mine arm.

'The harlot king' was the other part of his 'theame.'

But there yet remains the obsolete expression—

> but nothing
> Of his ill-ta'ne suspition.

To be something of is the same as *to be part of; i. e.*, to contribute to: and *to be nothing of* is not to contribute to. Thus, in *Antony and Cleopatra*, ii, 2, Antony says—

> Let this fellow
> Be nothing of our strife:

and Malone quotes from *Twelfth Night*, iii, 4, these words:

> Do me this courteous office, as to know of the knight, what my offence to him is: it is something of my negligence, nothing of my purpose.

V.—*Cymbeline*, act. iv, sc. 11.

Belarius, speaking of Cloten, says,

> Being scarse made up,
> I meane to man; he had not apprehension
> Of roaring terrors; For defect of judgement
> Is oft the cause of Feare. (Folio 1623.)

Theobald says of this, 'Cloten was defective in judgment, and therefore did not fear. Apprehensions of fear grow from a judgment in weighing danger: and a very easy change from the traces of the letters gives us this sense, and reconciles the reasoning of the whole passage.' So he proposes

> For *th' effect* of judgment
> Is oft the cause of fear:

and this exceedingly ingenious and intelligent emendation has met with almost universal adoption. Hanmer, however, retained 'defect' and read '*cure* of fear:' Staunton conjectured *sauce* for 'cause;' Dr. B. Nicholson, *loss;* Dr. Cartwright, *salve;* Professor Dowden, *cease;* and Mr. Joseph Crosby, *the act* for 'defect.' Knight, adopting an anonymous conjecture made in 1814, reads

> he had not apprehension
> Of roaring terrors for [*i. e.*, on account of] defect of judgment,
> *As* [being] oft the cause of fear:

which suggests to me the strained and creaking timbers of a vessel in a storm. Professor Sylvester was so good as to send me his interpretation of this disputed passage; and the moment I had read it such a flood of light burst upon my mind, that I instantly knew he had for ever redeemed the Folio text from emendation. I put his interpretation into form, adding to it some corroborative notes of my own, and sent it to Mr. Crosby, of Zanesville, the proposer of one of the above-recorded emendations. He withdrew his conjecture, and published my letter to him in *The American Bibliopolist* of October, 1876. The following is reprinted from that paper, with the addition of the two passages in *Richard III* and *Coriolanus*.

" The passage from *Cymbeline* seems to have stimulated your ingenuity rather than approved itself to your judgment. It is one of the most instructive in all Shakespeare, being one in which a phrase, *not in itself obsolete*, has lost the special sense it once had; and with the knowledge of that, the sense is absolutely perfect. The phrase in question is 'defect of judgment,' which all commentators have taken to mean *the total absence of judgment*, whereas it means *the defective use of judgment*. They were betrayed into this mistake by another; interpreting the phrase 'scarce made up to man' as if it referred to Cloten's youth ('before he arrived to man's estate,' says Knight), whereas Cloten was a middle aged man; and almost the same phrase is applied to *Richard III* (act i, sc. 1).

> Deform'd, unfinisht, sent before my time
> Into this breathing world, scarce half *made up*.

On the contrary, the phrase 'made up to man,' signified—in the full possession of a man's judgment; and when it is said that a certain person is 'scarce made up,' or 'scarce half made up,' it means that he had not *all his buttons*, or had not a man's judgment. Cloten, being scarce made up, took no heed of terrors that roared loud enough for men with their wits about them, and thus he braved danger; for it is the defective use of judgment (when men have any) which is oft the cause of fear. Compare the phrase 'defect of judgment' in *Coriolanus*, iv, 7,

> whether defect of judgment
> To fail in the disposing of those chances
> Which he was lord of;

and 'defects of judgment' in *Antony and Cleopatra*, ii, 2. A man without reason is fearless in the presence of imminent danger; a man with reason in perfection is equally fearless if his reason shows him the means of escape, for 'fear is nothing else but a betraying of the succours which reason offereth,' and therefore cannot be where reason is not. I am quoting from the *Wisdom of Solomon*, chap. xvii, verse 12."

I would add, there is no need for the most scrupulous reasoner to be solicitous about the logic of Belarius' reflection. 'For' is, indeed, the illative conjunction, but need not be strained to the full logical force. It is sufficient if the clause it introduces should have one of the senses of *as: q. d.* 'as, on the contrary, it is defect in that very faculty which Cloten's manhood had never reached, that is often the cause of fear in those who possess it.'

CHAPTER X.

THE SOULE ARAYED.*

He gave them their desire, and sent leanness withal into their souls.
Psalm cvi, 14.

ON a golden evening in August last [1871], for the first time in my life, I joined the gleaners in our own cornfields,—*nos, non nobis:* for, of course, I left my little sheaf with some of the daughters of toil who were gathering up the ears within the boundary of staves. To glean with the gleaners has great promise: but to glean after the gleaners has little or none. We know, to our cost, what it is to wade through the literature of Elizabeth and James; and also the delight of bearing off a scanty sheaf, of passages not yet utilized, for the elucidation or illustration of Shakespeare's text. He who gleans after the gleaners learns to be thankful for modest gains. Think how Lazarus would have fared if Dives had kept a dog upon

* This was a privately printed letter to Mr. Howard Staunton, in 1872.

the crumbs which fell from his table! Well: the editor of Shakespeare, who should depend upon the fruit of original research, would have but little advantage over such a beggar.

In these days, of all literary insects, it is the spider, not the bee, that makes a good thing of it.

In the fair fields of that literature the gleaning was done with the utmost vigilance and patience by that generation of critics who, from Steevens to Dyce, have thereby laid upon us so heavy a debt, but hitherto have been usually repaid by abuse. It has been the fashion to call them a *herd*, to dub them *criticasters*, to sneer at their dulness, and laugh at their verbosity. It is true that some of them might have done their work with more temper, othersome with less arrogance, and yet a few with better judgment or stricter integrity. But the labour was incurred, and the fruits of their study and research are our inheritance.

In the following pages I bring before you the evidences on which I have, as I believe, restored a line in Shakespeare's 146th Sonnet. A tractate devoted to the study of a single line will to many seem in the last degree absurd. That ingenious man, the late Mr. N. J. Halpin, was laughed at in *The Times* for having written a book on a single passage in *A Midsummer Night's Dream*: and I dare say many have made themselves merry at Mr. J. O. Phillipps' expense, for having written a pamphlet on a single line in *Cymbeline*. Critics need to have thick skins (more than one a piece, perhaps,) if they are to run the gauntlet at a Fools' Tourney. Our consolation is this: that we are quite capable of uniting the Artist and the Analyst, just as the sculptor knows the anatomy as well as feels the beauty of the human form. If we sometimes cannot 'see the wood for the trees,' we know that we have only to withdraw from the work of analysis to catch the glory of the whole. But however able we may be to appreciate that glory, it is our chosen walk to study the wood itself, I mean the *wood* which the ordinary spectator cannot see for the bark which covers it. It is, unfortunately, true that the timber has suffered excoriation and consequent decay, and that the exposed recesses have become the prey of an army of woodlice, who, if they had their way (I do not say their will), would make ruin of the old trees. It is the critic's duty to cleanse the corrupt recesses and to heal the breaches which have been made in the integrity of the timber. But none the less are we able to rejoice in that majesty which only looms at a distance.

In the case to which I now call your attention the gleaning was efficiently done nearly thirty years ago by Mr. Dyce; yet unlike Time, in Johnson's absurd lines, I did not 'toil after him in vain,' for I added an ear of corn to his sheaf. But through inattention to the requirements of the text, a remissness to which every critic is occasionally liable, it never occurred to him to question the purity of the *received* reading, nor to consider its relation to his own industry. The fact is that all collections of instances, in illustration of particular words and phrases, possess a potential virtue—an 'unknown worth,' like Love, in Shakespeare's 116th Sonnet.

The Sonnet to which I now wish to direct your attention is thus given in the 4to 1609.

146.

> Poore soule the center of my sinfull earth,
> My sinfull earth these rebbel powres that thee array,
> Why dost thou pine within and suffer dearth
> Painting thy outward walls so costlie gay?
> Why so large cost having so short a lease,
> Dost thou upon thy fading mansion spend?
> Shall wormes inheritors of this excesse
> Eate up thy charge? is this thy bodies end?
> Then soule live thou upon thy servants losse
> And let that pine to aggravat thy store;
> Buy tearmes divine in selling houres of drosse:
> Within be fed, without be rich no more,
> > So shalt thou feed on death, that feeds on men,
> > And death once dead, ther's no more dying then.

The second line of this Sonnet is allowed on all hands to be corrupt. It is not sense, and it is too long by two syllables. Now the repetition of the three words 'my sinful earth' naturally suggests the source of the corruption and a simple mode of cure. With one or two exceptions all the critics have treated those words at the beginning of the second line as a printer's reduplication. I wish I could say, *una litura potest:* but unfortunately the omission of those three words does not afford a perfect remedy, for the line is then deficient by two syllables. Malone supplied these by the words *Fool'd by*, reading

> Poor soul, the centre of my sinful earth,
> *Fool'd by those* rebel powers that thee array,

by which, of course, he meant that it was the soul, not the earth, that is so fooled. His selection of the verb was apparently determined by the following considerations. It is asked why the soul spends so much upon the decoration of a mansion which she must so soon quit. Now Malone took *arraying the soul* to mean *adorning the body* (!), and understood that the soul herself was induced to commit this wasteful vanity at the suggestion of certain rebel powers, to wit, the lusts of the flesh; for in that line it is *they* who are credited with the decoration! It is plain then that the soul is trepanned, tricked, or fooled by them. So he chose the last word because it adequately expresses this meaning, and—what is a most weighty consideration in emending so rhythmical a writer as Shakespeare —gives energy and melody to the verse. Malone's reading has been acquiesced in by nearly all subsequent editors. Even Mr. Dyce follows it, retaining, however, 'these' which Malone had altered into *those*. But it is founded on a foregone conclusion. Of course, if it be clearly conveyed in the unaltered sonnet that the rebel powers do stultify the soul in the matter of her raiment, the reading is admissible, if not actually justified. But so far from this being the case, apart from the second line, those powers are not once mentioned; but the soul herself is said to deck and paint *not herself* but her tenement. Meanwhile, then, what are the rebel powers about? What is it that usually occupies rebel powers? Surely not the decoration of the enemy's fortress, but *the consumption of the enemy's stores*, the siege, or the assault. It is one of those three destructive operations which one would have looked for in Shakespeare's line: and after all, is it not there?

These considerations preclude any such interpretation as Malone's. Before they occurred to me I had tried to supplement the defective line in many ways, supplying *e. g.*, *Foil'd by*, *Spoil'd by*, and *Sport of*. I afterwards found that Steevens had proposed to read

Starv'd by the rebel powers &c.,

that the author of *The Sonnets of Wm. Shakspere rearranged and divided into four parts* reads

Slave of these rebel powers &c.,

and that the Cambridge editors record an 'anon. conj.,' which runs thus,

Thrall to these rebel powers &c.

I have since encountered one of my own cast-offs in the *Gem Edition* of the Sonnets, where Mr. F. T. Palgrave reads,

Foil'd by the rebel powers &c.

I may add that an American critic (*Remarks on the Sonnets of Shakespeare*, [by E. A. H., of Washington City] 1865, p. 60) calls the rebel powers 'the arraigning powers;' by which expression he may possibly have intended a covert allusion to 'array:" but even he follows Malone's reading.

It was, I think, no slight gain to have perceived that Malone had forced on the second line an incongruous metaphor; that the rebel powers could not have been represented as putting raiment on the soul; for the soul's raiment is 'the muddy vesture of decay,' and that is not wrought by them, but too often destroyed by them: and that the supposition that they discharge so strange an office receives no support from the fourth line. It was, however, a far more important step to detect the required sense in the corrupt line.

I will relate how I came to take the second step. Mr. Dyce had elaborately prepared himself to make this discovery, years before I had studied the sonnet, by the most accurate discrimination of three verbs pronounced alike, whereof two (if not all three) have the same orthography. The word pronounced *array* is an equivoke for three distinct verbs.

(1) Array, to put raiment on anyone.
(2) Array, to put in array (or in battle-array).
(3) Aray, or array, to afflict or ill-treat.

Mr. Dyce had done more: he had collected seven early instances of the last verb; yet he failed to perceive that the verb in the corrupt line is not the first of those three verbs, nor yet the second, but the third!

Mr. Gerald Massey, in his big book on Shakespeare's Sonnets, made one step in the right direction; but unhappily made another in a wrong direction. He saw far more than Mr. Dyce. It was plain to him that the first *array* was not the verb used in that sonnet. But having reached this conclusion, he spoiled all by attempting to impose the second *array* on the corrupt line. This he did by retaining the three first words, which every critic had discarded as a reduplicative misprint, and the following is the text adopted by him:

> Poor soul, the centre of my sinful earth,—
> My sinful earth these rebel powers array—

Thus making the second line an impertinent parenthesis, and stultifying the demonstrative pronoun (these) by rejecting the only words which shew who the rebel powers are. What rebel powers? asks the reader; and here no answer is given in the text or by the critic. Besides this objection, every reader of taste must feel that the speaker having addressed his (or her) soul in the first line, preparatory to asking her, why she pines and starves within her fading mansion, would not have arrested the course of his (or her) thought by an interpolation having no connection, grammatical or substantive, with the rest of the sonnet. For my part, had the sonnet thus appeared in Thorpe's 4to, I should have marked it with an *obelus*: still less can I allow such writing to be imposed upon Shakespeare, when his publisher has not given it the sanction of print.

While thus condemning Mr. Massey's reconstruction, I honour him for having had one true insight. He saw that the maintenance and adornment of the soul's 'fading mansion' is not the direct work of the 'rebel powers' but of the soul herself. At the same time, I must add that his original insight seems to have suffered from his not perceiving that the verb *array* in that place cannot be an equivoke. His words are " These 'rebel powers' do not array the soul; they are of the flesh; they array his sinful earth. 'Array' here does not [only] mean dress, I think it [also] signifies that in the flesh these rebel powers set their battle in array against the soul" (*Shakespeare's Sonnets never before interpreted:* 1866, p. 379). The words I have put in square brackets should have been omitted. Their presence asserts that the *letters* a.r.r.a.y may stand for two distinct words. I take the last sentence of the extract as an *illustration*, not an *analysis*, of the proposed reconstruction; for of course he never could have believed that Shakespeare, had he written

> My sinful earth these rebel powers array,

intended *array* to be understood in the sense of

> Set (their) battle in array in—

i. e., in the flesh or sinful earth. If he did, however, I need offer him no apology for rescuing his reconstruction from a nonsensical interpretation.

A German critic, D. Barnstoff (*A Key to Shakespeare's Sonnets*, translated by T. J. Graham: 1862, p. 202), retaining the two words rejected by Mr. Massey, takes the verb *array* to mean

> Set (themselves) in array against—

for he makes Shakespeare paraphrase the second line (as it stands in Thorpe's 4to) in these words—'and by the term sinful earth I mean these human instincts, desires, passions, which set themselves in array against the noble ambition to excel.'

Having at length swept away all considerations supporting the assumption, that *array* in the 146th Sonnet means to *put raiment on*, or that it means to *set in array*, I proceed to consider the third interpretation: viz., that it means to *afflict* or *ill-treat*. In this sense *to aray*, or *array*, is an old word, seemingly cognate with *ray* and *beray;* and the three forms, 1. *aray*, 2. *ray*, 3. *beray*, mean pretty nearly the same thing, though it is still an unsettled question what is the radical concrete sense involved in them.

I note *en passant* that there are other verbs, *wray* and

bewray, *to disclose* or *manifest*.* These must not be confounded with *ray* and *beray*. The latter word is common: *e. g.*, 'but our fellow Shakespeare hath given him a purge, that made him *beray* his credit.' (*The Returne from Pernassus*, 1606. Act iv, sc. 3.) 'that * * lets his sonnes be plaine Ladies puppets, to *beray* a Ladies Chamber.' *Ibid.*, act ii, sc. 5. 'he that * * * makes a set speech to his greyhound, * * and if the dog * * * chance to *beray* the rome,' &c. *Ibid.*, act ii, sc. 6. 'yet they do nothing but *beray* my house.' *Ibid.*, act iii, sc. 2.

As to *aray*, Mr. Dyce and Mr. Joseph Payne err, in different directions, in assigning its radical meaning. Mr. Dyce (Edition of Skelton's *Works*, 1843, vol. ii, p. 196) says it means *to dispose of, to treat*. That is assuredly wrong. Mr. Payne (*Studies in English Prose*, 1868, p. 51) says it means *to soil with dirt*. While allowing that a physical sense is always more probable than an emotional sense, I must say this particular sense is not supported by any evidence. It is plain to me that the word is used by all writers in the fifteenth and sixteenth centuries to mean *to ill-treat;* and if that is only a 'second intention,' I do not think we have yet discovered the first. Can it be *to tear*

---

* Examples of both verbs abound in the Elizabethan literature, *e. g.*,

'With sugred words he *wraid* his sutes at fill.'
G. Whetstone's *Rock of Regard* (The Castle of Delight).

'Be not abasht the truth in wordes to *wray*.'
Ibid.

'And can those new Heads no new Will *bewray?*'
J. Davies' *Paper's Complaint*.

(*déchirer*)?* Two or three of the subsequent examples suggest this sense. Mr. Dyce founds his decision on Palsgrave's definition. '*Aray* condicion or case—*poynt.*' Mr. Payne founds his

> * This conjecture implies that the radical sense of *aray* is to *tear to strips*, or more generally *to shred*. In China it is the custom to *aray* their worst malefactors in this radical fashion: the criminal's flesh being *orayed*, *i. e.*, slashed, or cut into strips, before he is crucified. Dr. Sebastian Evans remonstrated with me upon a proposed etymology of this word; and the following remarks are extracted from his letter to me of Christmas, 1872.
>
> "A 'ray' is a *line*, or *streak*, more particularly a line or streak described from some centre or quasi-centre. Thus a hart 'runneth fast on his *raies*'— *i. e.*, lines of track; 'a bleeding hart the clean waves with purple gore did *ray*'—*i. e.*, streak with red rays; 'Grumio is *raied*'—*i. e.*, streaked all over with splashes, etc., etc. *Rayed*, in fact, came very often to mean *splashed*, and if you look at a splash you will see why. *Berayed* accordingly means *splashed*, and hence in a secondary sense *defiled*. Cf. in this connection to 'ray out,' *rayer de sang*, etc. Also, 'rayed with the yellows' as applied to a horse: as to which see *arragiato* in Florio's *New World of Words*, 'applied to a horse that hath the laske.'
>
> Now for *array*. It means—
> 1. to set in lines, rays, ranks, or rows.
> 2. to *arrange* in due order.
> 3. to *adorn* by arranging in due order.
> 4. (reflectively) to adorn oneself by arranging one's dress, etc., in due order.
> 5. (generically) to clothe or dress any person or thing.
> 6. to put any person or thing into a certain state, plight or predicament.
>
> I think this is the logical sequence of significances, but I don't exclude others which may be given, and I feel that throughout the series there runs a kind of under-current of meaning, conveying a sense of surrounding as with rays."

I may add that Chaucer employs the substantive in the Prologue to his *Canterbury Tales*, ll. 38—41, but apparently in the sense of *order*.

> To tellen you alle the condition
> Of eche of hem, so as it semed to me,
> And whiche they weren, and of what degre;
> And eke in what *araie* that they were inne:

on Palsgrave's example, 'Your gowne is foule arrayde;' and adds, 'The word is rare'—which it is not, but frequent with writers of those centuries. It became obsolete early in the seventeenth century. The following is Mr. Dyce's sheaf:

"WOFFULLY ARAID

Is mentioned by our author [John Skelton] as one of his compositions in the *Garlande of Laurell*, v, 1418, vol. i, 417.
With the opening of this piece compare Hawes's *Convercyon of Swerers*, where Christ is made to exclaim,

> 'They newe agayne do hange me on the rode,
> They tere my sydes, and are nothynge dysmayde,
> My woundes they do open, and devoure my blode:
> I, god and man, moost *wofully arayde*,
> To you complayne, it maye not be *denayde;*
> Ye nowe to lugge me, ye tere me at the roote,
> Yet I to you am chefe refuyte and bote.'

and a little after,

> 'Why arte thou *harde herted*, &c. Sig. A iii, ed. n. d. 4to.

Barclay too has,

> 'Some sweareth armes, nayles, heart, and body,
> Tearing our Lorde worse then the Jewes him *arayde*.'
> *The Ship of Fooles*, fol. 33, ed. 1570.

Woffully araid is, I believe, equivalent to—wofully disposed of or treated, in a woful condition. '*Araye* condicion or case—*poynt*.' Palsgrave's Lesclar. de la Lang. Fr., 1530, fol. xviii. (Table of Subst.)—(and see note, p. 164, v. 163.)

> '*Isaac.*—What have I done, fader, what have I saide?
> *Abraham.*—Truly, no kyns ille to me.
> *Isaac.*—And thus gyltles shalle be *arayde*.'
> Abraham,—Towneley Mysteries, p. 40.

'His [Tybert's] body was al to beten, and blynde on the one eye.

Whan the kynge wyste this, that tybert was thus *arayed*, he was sore angry,' &c.—*Reynard the Fox*, sig. b 8, ed. 1481. Again, in the same romance,* when Isegrym the wolf has received a kick on the head from a mare, he says to Reynard, 'I am so foule *arayed* and sore hurte, that an herte of stone might have pyte of me.'— Sig. f 4.

> 'Who was wyth love : more *wofully arayed*
> Than were these twayne.'
> Hawes's *Pastime of Pleasure*, sig. I iiii, ed. 1555.

'I am fowle *arayed* with a chyne cowgh. *Laceor* pertussi.'—He was sore *arayed* with sycknesse. Morbo atrociter *conflictus est*.'
Hormanni *Vulgaria*, sigs. II iii, I ii, ed. 1530."

To this sheaf, as I have said, I was enabled to add but one ear (not counting the passage in Shakespeare's 146th Sonnet), viz.,

'And on the morowe erly the ten men of armes came tofore the daulphyn alle wounded and sore hurt. And they recounted to hym how two yonge men onely had *arayed* them so and how they nedes must flee for fere of theyr lyves.'—*Paris and Vienna*, 1459, Caxton. Reprint, 1868. Roxburgh Library, p. 47.

Richardson seems to me to go astray in giving, as the radical meaning of *aray*, ' to cover, to cloak, to dress, to set in order;' by which error he is naturally led to assign, as the signification of *ray* or *beray* (as Mr. Payne did, after him, of *aray*), ' to cover with dirt,' ' to dirty, to befoul, to bespatter with dirt.' He quotes, however, two examples apparently in point from Spenser's *Faery Queen* :

---

* From 'Isegrym the Wolf's Experiment in Reading.' 'Alas, Reynart! alas! said the wolf, I pray you to leve your mockyng. I am so foule *arayed*,' &c.

>   'And the cleane waves with purple gore did *ray*.'
>
>   B. ii, c. 1.
>
>   '[Wypt] from his face the filth that did it *ray*.'
>
>   B. vi, c. 5.

Of the form (abbreviated or radical, whichever it may turn out to be) *ray*, two examples occur in the *Taming of the Shrew*, iii, 2, and iv, 1, thus:

>   'His horse * * * *raied* with the yellowes.'
>   'Was ever man so beaten? was ever man so *raide?*'

In these two passages Mr. Dyce interpreted the participle, by comparing it in the former case with *berayed*, and in the latter with *arayed;* and he explains it as 'in evil condition, afflicted.' With all this apparatus of learning, however, he failed to perceive that when Shakespeare says,

> ——— 'these rebel powers that thee [the soul] *array*,'

he is using exactly the same word; for it is just the lusts of the flesh that (in the words of the Collect) 'assault and hurt the soul,' *i. e., array* the soul by consuming that store which has been already impoverished by her lavish expenditure on that which profits her nothing.

I hold it therefore fully established that 'array' in this sonnet means *ill-treat*, or *bring to an evil condition*. This conclusion seems to necessitate another. Discarding the first three words as an error of the press, it becomes evident that the use of the pronoun 'thee' in the defective line is conclusive against the reflexion of the leading words to the soul. This is a matter to be felt rather than reasoned out. If I could believe that those words refer to the soul I should read,

Heart of these rebel powers that thee aray.

But even then, though I should evade the truism that Malone's reading and others should foist into the line, the structure would still be awkward. I most strongly *feel* that the leading words must have a direct application to the proximate substantive, 'earth,' and that the second line must be a justification of the expression 'sinful earth,' which is otherwise out of relation with the entire sonnet. I *feel* also that the second line ought to be to the following effect:

> *Sinful* earth, because it harbours powers that rebel against the
> Soul, and are therefore sinful.

Now here I will be careful not to speak *dogmaticé*, there being so few *data* in the problem. Take the substantive *seat* tentatively, and you will perfectly understand the reading I desiderate in that line. Had Shakespeare written

> *Seate of* these rebbel powres that thee aray

all would have been satisfactory, and the reading would have received illustration from the 109th Sonnet, where the bard says—

> Never believe, though in my nature reign'd
> All frailties that *besiege* all kinds of blood, &c.

But it still seems that a more satisfactory sense would be imparted to the passage if the earth were treated as the *accomplice*, than as the *residence*, of the rebel powers. While I was endeavouring to restore the defective line, with a view to this sense, Mr. A. E. Brae (who had been independently studying the sonnet) communicated to me a correction which had at length occurred to him, viz., *Leagu'd with:* so that the first two lines would run thus:

> Poor soul, the centre of my sinful earth,
> *Leagued with* these rebel powers that thee aray,

which reading strikes me as fulfilling every condition of the case: it is the earth that is in league with the rebel powers, and the earth itself is therefore called 'sinful.' Here we have the flesh represented as leagued or compacted with its carnal desires in the work of defrauding the soul of her rightful nutriment, whereby she pines within and suffers dearth.

END.

Intercalary Notes.

—o—

P. 36. I should have added, that Bishop Percy's interleaved copy of Langbaine, in 4 vols., is now in the possession of Mr. A. Holt White, of Clements Hall, Rochford.

P. 57. Note.—To the list of books on the Shakespeare and Bacon Controversy, should be added, *Shakespeare: from an American Point of View; including an Inquiry into his Religious Faith and his Knowledge of Law: with the Baconian Theory considered, by George Wilkes.* 1877.

P. 61. Exactly so, it is an argument against Shakespeare's authorship of *The Merry Devil of Edmonton* (4to, 1631), that there are in it passages which resemble Shakespeare: *e. g.*,

> My stiffened haire stands upright on my head,
> As doe the bristles of a Porcupine.

P. 105. To the references to *Notes and Queries*, 5th S., given in note on p. 59, should be added, vi, 370; vii, 213; vii, 316.

P. 143, line 12. 'Very foolishly.' Mr. Hugh Carleton, of New Zealand, writes me word that, in his opinion, 'foolishly' here means *stolidly*. He may very well be right. It is also worth a note that, in the previous part of the same scene, the 'fool i' the forest' is represented by Jaques as having made some exceedingly trite remarks 'very wisely,' where the qualification appears to mean the same as in the passage under consideration.

P. 152. Mr. F. J. Furnivall insists upon it, that the two propositions,

> Being scarse made up,
> I mean to man; he had not apprehension
> Of roaring terrors:

and

> Defect of judgement
> Is oft the cause of Feare:

though connected by the illative conjunction 'for,' are not associated as result and condition; and he challenges me to give the logical forms in which they stand. The forms are —

> All not-Ys are not-Xs,
> Since, All Xs are Ys.

Belarius, however, contents himself with stating the particular converse of the latter proposition: viz.,

> Some Ys are Xs,

the particularity being marked by the word 'oft:' a reason for which may be found in the imperfect recognition this great psychological fact has received from the critics of the text.

Of course Mr. Furnivall, or anyone, may so interpret the two propositions as to save them from these forms: but, if 'for' is to be taken in its full logical force, into these forms they must go; and surely it is better that they should go into them, or that 'for' should not be so taken, than that the text of the Folio should be altered to suit 'the taste and fancy' of the critic. Besides, 'what is sauce for the goose is sauce for the gander,' and Mr. Furnivall ought in consistency and *a fortiori* to demur to the following text in St. John viii, 47,

> He that is of God heareth God's words:
> Ye *therefore* hear them not, because ye are not of God.

P. 166, line 6. Observing the verb *ray* in John Davies' *Paper's Complaint*, 1620, p. 230, where Paper says,

> One *raies* me with course Rimes;

and seeing *infra*, p. 237,

> But that which most my Soule *excruciates*, &c.,

and p. 242,

> This, this (O this) my *rexed* Soule doth kill!

I concluded that *ray* in the former line meant *to excrnciate, to vex*, &c. But on reading the intermediate part of that foolish poem, I saw that I was, not improbably, on a false scent, and that *ray=dress*.

> Yet, Poets love I, sith they made me weare
> (What weares out Time) my rich, and gaudiest Geare.
> Yea, those I love that in too earnest Game
> (or little Spleene) did me no little shame.
> Sith I can witnesse to succeeding Times
> They oft have me *araid* with royall Rimes,
> That ravish Readers (though they envious bee,)
> Such sacred Raptures they have put on me.

Printed by JOSIAH ALLEN, Birmingham.

SHAKESPEARE'S CENTURIE OF PRAYSE (1592-1693), being Materials for a History of Opinion on Shakespeare and His Works, culled from Writers of the first Century after his rise, collected and edited, (with elucidations), by C. M. Ingleby, LL.D., *printed on thick hand-made paper, in old style type, large paper with facsimile,* 4to, *bound in boards, in the antique style,* £2. 2s.

1874.

—— *small paper, in paper wrapper, uniform in style with the Spencer Society Publications,* 21s.   1874.

Trübner & Co., 57 & 59, Ludgate Hill.

Opinions of the Press.

Mr. W. MINTO: in the *Examiner*, January 16, 1875.

IT seems at first sight that it would be easy enough to collect all that can be found about Shakespeare in the writings of a given period, more especially when generations of scholars have gone over the ground and recorded their discoveries. But any investigator who, like Dr. Ingleby, resolves to go over the ground again, and glean references hitherto undetected, has a sufficiently laborious task before him, and one in which the dry research is relieved and rewarded at rare intervals. * * Dr. Ingleby remarks in his preface that he had little conception of the difficulties of his work till he had advanced some way towards its execution. Although he modestly disclaims absolute completeness for his collection, and expects that there are still many gleanings to be had, there can be no doubt that his 'Centurie of Prayse' is all but theoretically complete, and certainly complete enough to afford reasonable satisfaction to all who are interested in the question that he has proposed to illustrate. * * * It is interesting in itself, and it may be made a most fertile basis for reflection and speculation.

Opinions of the Press.

The late Mr. RICHARD SIMPSON: in the *Academy*, February 6, 1875.

DR. Ingleby's very careful compilation is meant to include almost all the passages alluding to Shakspere which occur in books or writings between 1592 and 1693. * * * The series of Shakspere Allusion-books which Dr. Ingleby is publishing for the New Shakspere Society is nearly the same in design as the present work, the difference being that the series professes to give the whole or an integral portion of the books, while the *Centurie of Prayse* gives only the passages in which the allusions occur. Dr. Ingleby, in a modest preface, states the difficulty of his task, and the unlikelihood that the first attempt to attain completeness should be entirely successful. Indeed, when the whole literature of a hundred years has to be searched, it is hard to see when the collection can be pronounced complete: there may lurk so many allusions which want an Œdipus to unriddle, so many obscure passages may have been wrongly tacked on to Shakspere; and so many rare books or manuscripts may still be extant which have not been read by any one sufficiently on the look-out for such passages. * * * To know the earlier criticism Dr. Ingleby's book is indispensable.

Notes and Queries, February 13, 1875.

DR. Ingleby had a 'happy thought' when the idea of preparing a work like the present first offered itself to his mind. It is one lacking which no Shakspearian library can pretend to be perfect. Dr. Ingleby gives brief passages from books whose authors wrote between 1592 and 1693. Each passage refers to Shakspeare, not invariably in praise of him, but always in proof of the hold which the national poet had on the heart or judgment of the nation. * * * Each passage collected by Dr. Ingleby serves as a link in the life of the poet. A second passage is never given on the same page, but some extracts occupy several pages. There is 'ample room and verge enough' for possessors of the volume to make annotations in the margin; and the printing is creditable to the press of Josiah Allen, of Birmingham. * * * The danger [of Shakspeare's depreciation], indeed, exists no longer; and Dr. Ingleby's book will help to keep it from reviving, for it proves (a little, perhaps, against that accomplished gentleman's own opinion) that Shakspeare was in the hearts of the people from the very first, and that with the restoration of the monarchy he was permanently re-enthroned, *semper floreat*.

The *Saturday Review*, March 6, 1875.

DR. Ingleby's collection of Shakspearian criticisms, panegyrics, and allusions is a book of luxury; but it is something more than a mere book of luxury. In that character indeed it leaves nothing to desire. Some of the pieces here collected are merely curious or odd, giving evidence of nothing beyond the fact that particular works of Shakspeare were well enough known to the writers to be the subject of passing mention. But the main scope of the book is such as to take it out of the class of mere literary curiosities. The men of Shakspeare's own time and the times next following it tell us here in their own words what they thought of him. We have the judgments of his fellow-poets, sometimes expressed by themselves, sometimes reported at secondhand by collectors of anecdote, the panegyrics of friends, and the sneers of his few enemies. The editor's notes supply concisely but sufficiently such things as are needful for the understanding of the less obvious points. We confess that we should have liked a little more discussion and justification of some extracts which on the face of them are doubtful, but the fault is on the right side. * * * Dr. Ingleby's conclusion from the evidence is that Shakspeare's own age admired him much, but not adequately. He says that no one during the 'Centurie' (that is, the century after Shakspeare began to publish) had any suspicion that the genius of Shakspeare was unique. This is in some measure true, but we think it is over-stated. That Shakspeare had not in his own generation that sort of classical fame which no man can have till after his death, one may of course readily admit ; that it was not foreseen by any one then how much he would overshadow his contemporaries in the eyes of posterity, seems also probable enough, if not certain ; but that the peculiar qualities of his genius—those, in fact, which make it, as Dr. Ingleby says, unique—were to a considerable extent seen and appreciated from the first, we think is fairly made out by the witnesses here collected. Doubtless one must not be misled by the wording of their praise, although the words are often as strong, and perhaps as apt, as any we could find now that we are supposed to know Shakspeare so much better. In those days the language of both praise and blame was much less guarded than it is at present, and the sort of reserve which modern manners impose on us, even in speaking well of living persons, did not exist. Epithets and flowers of speech must be taken as standing in themselves for less than they would stand for now. But, after allowing for all this, we find evidence of a real discernment and sympathy quite incompatible with the notion of Shakspeare's being, in the eyes of the best wits of his time, only one of a number of more or less respectable poets and playwrights of whom for various reasons it was desirable to speak civilly.

The *Athenæum*, March 20, 1875.

In a volume, on which he has bestowed the quaint title of 'Shakespeare's Centurie of Prayse,' Dr. Ingleby has collected so many of these and other references as occurred within a hundred years of the commencement of Shakspeare's fame, from the close of 1592, that is, to 1693. In the dearth of other and more exact information, these 'Materials for a History of Opinion on Shakespeare and his Works' are not without value. With a few exceptions, however, the criticisms, when such are passed, are only remarkable as evincing how far were contemporaries in general from rightly estimating the size of the man with whom they dwelt. The praise lavished upon him is of the kind which is bestowed upon those of his contemporaries who were most popular with their fellows. * * * To reprint all the slurs of which incapacity has been guilty is a whimsical task. Something may, however, in the case of Shakspeare, concerning whom we know so little, be urged in its favour, and the task has been thoroughly accomplished. Fresh references to Shakspeare turn up as the by-paths of literature are

Opinions of the Press.

more fully explored. Dr. Ingleby's work will not, accordingly, long remain complete. * * * It is, however, a creditable result of industry and research.

Professor HIRAM CORSON: in the *Cornell Review*, May, 1875.

THAT William Shakespeare, of Stratford-upon-Avon, Gent., was the author of these Dramas, every one who is willing to accept testimony thereunto pertaining, equally strong and conclusive as the testimony that is requisite in a civilized court of justice, to hang a man, can find such testimony in abundance in the volume before us. He who would reject the testimony it affords, could not consistently accept the testimony bearing upon the authorship of the Canterbury Tales, the Faerie Queene, the Paradise Lost, the Rape of the Lock, the Task, or any other well-known product of English Literature.

But let it not be inferred, from the above remarks, that it is a purpose of the 'Centurie of Prayse' to furnish such testimony. There is not the slightest allusion thereto, and such a thing doesn't appear to have been in the editor's mind. But the work *does* furnish it, nevertheless. * * *

To return to the work before us. The leading purpose that the editor had in view, in its preparation, was, as set forth in the title, to offer 'materials for a history of opinion on Shakespeare and his works, culled from writers of the first century after his rise;' that is, from 1592, the 28th year of his age, to 1693; and these materials are far more abundant than any who have not made a special study of the subject, and who hold the traditional opinion that little or nothing has been delivered of Shakespeare by his contemporaries, would be apt to suppose. The Index to Authors cited, contains 116 names, a large number of them being those of prominent writers; Anonymous Works, 25; List of Exclusions (I. Irrelevant Allusions, 11; II. Spurious Allusions, 5), 16; and in a Postscript are given the titles of 8 plays, published from 1599 to 1662, which show an influence of Shakespeare's works. In the 'Forespeech' the editor states that he 'has excluded from the catena all documentary notices of Shakespeare; for, besides being foreign to its scope, they are sufficiently numerous and extensive to form a considerable volume by themselves.'

SHAKESPEARE HERMENEUTICS, OR THE STILL LION, being an Essay towards the Restoration of Shakespeare's Text. By C. M. Ingleby, LL.D. *Printed in all respects to range with* SHAKESPEARE'S CENTURIE OF PRAYSE, *and bound in boards, in the same style*, 6s. 1875.

Trübner & Co., 57 & 59, Ludgate Hill.

Opinions of the Press.

Dr. FRIEDRICH V. BODENSTEDT: in the *Jahrbuch* of the German Shakespeare Society for 1867. (Preface, p. viii.)

INGLEBY, to whom we are indebted for the most complete view and exposure of the Shakespeare Forgeries, which made so much stir in the world at their time, gives us here, as the precursor of a larger work [*Shakespeare Hermeneutics*], contributions for the restoration of the Shakespearian text. I have considered it unnecessary to translate his essay, because the principal contents of it would, even in a German dress, remain unintelligible to any one not acquainted with the English language.

The *Saturday Review* (on first sketch), July 20, 1867.

UNDER the eccentric title of *The Still Lion*, Dr. Ingleby indites an essay on the conjectural emendation of the Text, which abounds in robust, pithy sense, jocose humour, and felicitous illustration. There is also enough personality to remind us that the Shakespearian critics of this country are a quarrelsome brood.

Mr. F. J. FURNIVALL's *Introduction to Gervinus' Commentaries*, 1874, p. xlvi.

DR. Ingleby describes his just publisht *Still Lion* as 'indications of a systematic Hermeneutic [science of interpretation] of Shakspere's text.' It is strongly against plausible emendations, and is well worth study.

A A

Opinions of the Press.

Mr. JOSEPH CROSBY: in the *American Bibliopolist*, April, 1875.

As an ancillary contribution to this study, the clever essay, named at the head of this article, deserves more than a passing notice. * * * From the well-considered principles it lays down for the restoration, and just interpretation, of the Text of Shakespeare; the happy expositions of many obscure and difficult passages brought out in the illustration of these principles, and the charming and often harmonious style of the author, we venture to say it will be greedily and gratefully welcomed by every earnest student of the poet. * * * In two noteworthy respects this essay differs from most books of criticism: the author keeps clear of any attempt to display his own acuteness, or powers of satire, under the garb of elucidating Shakespeare; and albeit every page is replete with originality, sound criticism, and learning, it is so lighted up with good sense, humor, and frequent illustrations, that there is not a line of dry reading in the book. * * * Every sentence bristles with good points. The pen in his hand is a polished weapon, and he deals his blows right and left on all impertinent correctors and blundering restorers of the Text, from Mr. Perkins-Ireland down to Mr. Staunton in his late 'Unsuspected Corruptions,' in a style that is at once vigorous and trenchant, and very amusing. * * * We beg, again, heartily to thank Dr. Ingleby for his masterly little volume; and to express the hope that every intending editor of Shakespeare will ponder well, and profit by, the sound doctrine it inculcates. Nothing but good—much good—can result from a careful study of its too few pages.

The *Athenæum*, October 9, 1875.

DR. INGLEBY is entitled to a prominent place in the ranks of those who have taken up the task of the elucidation of Shakspeare, and his work is one of the most scholarly and important contributions yet made to Shakspearean literature. * * * Although separated from the average commentator by gifts of perception and temper, Dr. Ingleby is still of the race. He is unable quite to resist an inclination towards the conjecture he condemns, or to treat with the amused indifference which they merit the framers of absurd suggestions. If, like Narcissa, whose nature

> moderately mild,
> To make a wash would hardly stew a child,

he will not condemn his predecessors to the kind of fate heresy in matters of critical opinion is supposed to merit, he will not let them pass entirely scatheless, but will subject them to some form of comic torture. * * * Quite incontrovertible are the canons [of emendation] Dr. Ingleby advances, and an observance of them would winnow to a very small heap the mountain of Shakspeare hermeneutics.

Notes and Queries, October 30, 1875.

THIS is the text on which Dr. Ingleby gives half-a-dozen or so of the best Shakspeare sermons we have ever read. He certainly proves, in a variety of cases, that critics and commentators have often been miserably ignorant of the very elements of the science which they affected to interpret or illustrate as so many Sir Oracles, at the opening of whose mouths no dog was to dare to bark. Nothing, in its way, can be more amusing than Dr. Ingleby's dealing with words in Shakspeare which are perfectly unintelligible to everybody. He shows the various conflicting words which critics have proposed to substitute for them, and then demonstrates beyond gainsaying that the proposed substitutes are, in truth, incomprehensible, and that Shakspeare used terms perfectly natural, forming current coins of speech in his time, and pregnant with meaning when translated into the forms used in ours. In many other respects Dr. Ingleby's boldly written and masterly book recommends itself to Shakspearian (and indeed to all) readers. He does full justice to skilled commentators; but seldom has the crowd of incompetent critics been more mauled, bruised, knocked down, and danced over, than by Dr. Ingleby.

The *Examiner*, November 20, 1875.

DR. Ingleby has framed a powerful defence of Shakespeare against the extravagance of conjectural emendators under the somewhat odd and fantastic title of 'The Still Lion.' * * * For years a strong feeling has been growing up in favour of a more reverent and scholarly treatment of the text, and Dr. Ingleby's vigorous polemic should help greatly to promote this feeling. * * *

In his last chapter, in which he impresses us still more with the width and accuracy of his reading, and the strength and sagacity of his critical sense, Dr. Ingleby lays down certain restrictions under which he would permit the reformed emendator to look for an honest living. * * * Under these restrictions, rigorously enforced, the emendator might indeed do comparatively little harm to anything but the temper of his reader, but it would probably be for the advantage of all concerned if for the next fifty years he would consent to hang his harp upon the willows, and study Shakespeare no more.

Mr. H. H. FURNESS: in *Lippincott's Magazine*, March, 1876.

THE lion's slumbers were here [*i. e.*, in passages in which the word *help* has been superseded] of the lightest, and happy men be our dole to have escaped with whole skins. Thus Dr. Ingleby takes up passage after passage of Shakespeare that has been pronounced corrupt, and shows that the fault imputed to it lies not in the text, but in the lack of requisite knowledge, be it of language, of usage, of manners and customs, or even of Elizabethan spelling and grammar, on the part of the critic. The mischief that ignorance has done in the past is irrevocable, but such impressive warnings as Dr. Ingleby gives us may *help*, in both senses of the word [*i. e.*, aid and cure], in the future. * * * Great as is the service done in particular cases, the most valuable part of *The Still Lion* is the moral which it points, that 'successful emendation is the fruit of severe study and research on the one hand, and of rare sensibility and sense on the other;' and in our opinion Dr. Ingleby might have gone even farther, and demanded for it a spark of that creative power which is genius.

Opinions of the Press.

Professor HIRAM CORSON: in the *Cornell Review*, May, 1876.

IT must be a source of gratification to every Shakespeare scholar who has any reverence for 'Mr. William Shakespeares Comedies, Histories, and Tragedies, published according to the True Originall Copies,' to read the evidence which this work affords, of an approach towards a *science* of interpretation and emendation, in lieu of the arbitrary cutting and slashing to which all the editors of the Poet's works have, for nearly two hundred years, been more or less addicted.

Professor DOWDEN: in the *Academy*, September 16, 1876.

DR. Ingleby's conservative criticism, his maintenance of the original text in various difficult passages, is highly ingenious, and in not a few instances is decisively successful. Even the reader who is not a special student of the text of Shakspere cannot fail to enjoy the keen and swift coursing of the critic's intellect after truth, which doubles but does not escape. When the famous greyhound, Master Magrath, was anatomised it was ascertained that the extraordinarily swift action of the limbs was due to the enormous relative size of the heart. In like manner it is often the inner imagination which quickens and sustains action that outwardly appears to us wholly intellectual; the imagination is the blood-propelling organ. And thus it is with Dr. Ingleby. A chapter might well have been added on 'Hygiene of the textual critic.' Each occupation has its special diseases. * * * In a similar way a textual *crux* plays tricks with the eye that has stared upon it too long. It is thus that we must account for the extraordinary follies in the way of textual criticism perpetrated by very clever men. The mental eye became affected somewhat as Turner's sense of sight is alleged by an eminent oculist to have been. And besides this, there are certain diseases constitutional rather than local, to which the verbal critic is exposed. Some one of the craft should study the pathology of his peculiar guild and mystery. And it would be satisfactory to know the means by which W. Sidney Walker, and Dr. Ingleby himself, were enabled to keep their faculties all in good form, and in a state of mutually quickening activity.

Printed by JOSIAH ALLEN, Birmingham.

www.ingramcontent.com/pod-product-compliance
Lightning Source LLC
Chambersburg PA
CBHW020244170426
43202CB00008B/221